P9-AQO-715

WITHDRAWN

INNOCENCE and POWER

Individualism in Twentieth-Century America

INNOCENCE *and* POWER

Individualism in Twentieth-Century America

EDITED WITH AN INTRODUCTION BY GORDON MILLS

AUSTIN UNIVERSITY OF TEXAS PRESS

CARL A. RUDISILL LIBRARY
LENOIR RHYNE COLLEGE
HICKORY, N. C. 28601

301
M62i
92443
Feb. 1975

Library of Congress Catalog Card No. 63–63658
Copyright © 1965 by the University of Texas Press
All Rights Reserved
Manufactured in the United States of America

CONTENTS

INTRODUCTION

Individualism, although casually singular in implication, is in experience more nearly a myriad of spokes in a wheel jolting over new ground. Sometimes, indeed, it is a wheel of fire.

The spokes of a wheel suggest polarities, and multiplicity. If one pole is complete passivity to the will of other people, or to the force of institutions, the opposite is total disregard of any will except one's own. Most of us live our lives, and define our individualities, at some point on the interval between these two extremes. The hub of society for the rational, humane man is the principle of a tolerable balance, one that is both moral in its restraint and creative in its freedom and opportunity. Individualism as an everyday matter is a relationship, the stance an individual takes within his community. Were there no neighbors, no other life, a man could scarcely tell of what his individualism consisted. He would be only an individual, not in any sense an individualist—unless, like St. Thomas Aquinas, he engaged in intricate speculation upon his relationship to God.

For practical purposes we should use the plural: individualisms. The conceivable number and variety must be almost infinite, and the demands upon our judgment are incessant. At breakfast, Citizen X gloomily revolves in his mind the question of individualism in respect to his family's desire to give a party. He yields. On his way to work he expresses a sturdy individualism at the wheel of his car, in traffic. During the morning he reluctantly conforms to his business associates' desire to issue a public statement denouncing encroachments by the federal government. At four o'clock in the afternoon he talks gently with a somewhat paranoiac employee who believes Citizen X is trying to make him do more than his share of the work. At eight in the evening, in defiance of the wishes of his wife, he takes an aggressive part in a poker game. Is he an individualist?

Pondering the question, we note at once that Citizen X is to some degree an individualist simply because of his relationships with other people, relationships less primitive than utter passivity or mindless violence. Next we recognize that consideration of the question can, for convenience, be broken down into two broad areas. One is an analysis of the kinds of relationships in which it may be said individualism is being asserted, usually followed by value judgments about these relationships. The other is an examination of evidence concerning possible limitations on freedom of choice, and finally, perhaps, on the meaning of the concept of choice itself. Such evidence might be legal, economic, physiological, psychological, metaphysical, and so on.

Having posed this staggering multiplicity of problems, any sensible man would flee, if he had any place to flee to. The demands are too great. I think it might be agreed that, by comparison, nuclear physics offers only moderate difficulty, atomic structure being, after all, apparently simpler than the structure of the human personality. But one of the salient features of the historic American experience seems to have been the shock of discovering that there is no place to go. For many individual Americans this discovery, or the lifelong knowledge of this simple fact, has been an experience of great pain: for the homesteader whose land was taken from him; for the Negro; for the European immigrant snared in the slums of New York or Chicago. It once was thought that in the aboriginal wilderness of the American continent a new innocence would be found, and a remnant of this idea still gallops grotesquely across our TV screens each evening. The American is a new man, said Crèvecoeur. Like the deserts of the Holy Land, the wilderness beckoned the prophet to come and find God, or himself; and Americans praised God for their remoteness from the teeming slums of Europe. There was much truth in these attitudes, but the truth was never so simple as the notion of an innocent individualism secured through the beneficence of unspoiled nature. And now, with nuclear power looking over our shoulder at our every move, the sad destiny of the idea that the spaciousness of the American continent might prove a refuge for such an individualism seems to have been figured forth in Rölvaag's pathetic character Beret, in *Giants in the Earth*. Taken from her native Norway to a homestead on the plains of western America, the land of the big sky, she slowly went mad, obsessed with the thought that there was no place to hide.

There is no refuge from the problems of individualism, and there is likewise no apparent hope for their final "solution." Even were finally satisfactory answers to our questions found today, many of them would surely have lost their force by tomorrow. New conditions, some of them probably created by the very act of giving answers, would require fresh examination and previously untried personal adjustments. Yet it appears that something may be done, especially since many of us who read the essays in this book—although surely not all of us—will do so in relative safety, enjoying at least the impression that we are thinking our thoughts and taking our actions with a certain amount of creative freedom.

Concerning what has been done and may be done, and must be done, we necessarily turn for illumination to a broad group of disciplines within our intellectual life—not forgetting, meanwhile, our historic indebtedness to harassed, sometimes simple, men of action. We are particularly fortunate in the high distinction of the minds represented in the following essays; beyond this, we are fortunate in their bringing with them the resources of six different disciplines. Out of the fascinating shifting of perspectives among these essays, with their reassuring areas of agreement, and stimulating or disturbing points of failure to agree, the inevitable inference is strongly drawn again that knowledge is seamless even if our habits of thought are not.

Five of these essays were read at a meeting on individualism held by the American Studies Association of Texas, and sponsored by The University of Texas, in December 1962. These five essays were first published in the Summer 1963 issue of the *Texas Quarterly.* They have since undergone various degrees of revision. In the present publication the essays by Clarence Ayres and Charles Hartshorne appear for the first time.

The December 1962 conference and the subsequent publication of these essays have altogether required the support and assistance of many individuals. I hope they will share my own feeling of pleasure and satisfaction in what has been done. On their behalf, and my own, I should like to express here a special gratitude to Mody C. Boatright, J. Alton Burdine, and Harry H. Ransom, whose long-continued support and encouragement have been indispensable to the development of American studies in the Southwest.

GORDON MILLS

Deep Creek Lake, Maryland

INNOCENCE *and* POWER
Individualism in Twentieth-Century America

◇◇◇

Individuality and Individualism
A Culturological Interpretation

BY LESLIE A. WHITE

THIS PAPER UNDERTAKES an inquiry into the nature of individuality, and reviews doctrines of individualism well entrenched in contemporary American thought, especially in anthropological theory.

An individual is a distinguishable member of a class of things or events. One member of a class can be distinguished from others by its discreteness on the one hand and by its particular features on the other. But, even if members of a class had no particular features, their very discreteness would give each an individuality. An atom of copper would have individuality even if it were exactly like every other atom of copper. But no two atoms are exactly alike, just as no two peas or mice or men are exactly alike. And we could not speak of two things being exactly alike, or of *two things* at all, if they were not distinguishable discretely. We see individuality, therefore, in its relationship to continuum and to particular characteristics. Given complete likeness, theoretically, individuality is realized through discreteness. Given discreteness, individuality may be further expressed through particular characteristics.

But the factor of discreteness is not as simple as it appears at first glance. Viewed superficially, a thing or event may appear to be discrete or not-discrete, with no intermediate positions. Sometimes this is the case, but it is not always so. The individuality of a brick is determined by its discreteness and by its intrinsic properties; its individuality is not determined by its relationship to other bricks except insofar as it is a member of a class.

But it is otherwise with living organisms. An ape is an ape, but his individuality is affected by his relationships with other apes. These relationships are of two kinds: genetic and sociological. As a physical object, his discreteness is entire and complete. As a biological organism, his discreteness is complete in one respect but not in another. He is a complete, autonomous whole, and he could continue to exist even if all other apes were suddenly extinguished. But as a biological organism, his discreteness is not entire and complete; his individuality has been affected by the organisms of his forebears. He is what he is because his genetic composition has been determined by those of his parents, and by their parents in turn. He is both a genotype and a phenotype; his individuality is a function of both phylogeny and ontogeny.

The individuality of an ape is, therefore, of a different order from that of a brick. The individuality of the latter is wholly a matter of discreteness within a uniformity of a class of things. The individuality of the former is the product of a qualified discreteness and of variation among the members of the class. But the important thing, for our present purposes, is that the individuality of a brick, insofar as it arises from particular characteristics rather than from mere membership in a class, is not affected, or determined, by other bricks, whereas the biological individuality of the ape *is* profoundly affected by other apes.

Individuality among apes is affected by their interrelationships on a sociopsychological level as well as upon a biological level.

The individuality of an ape is determined not only by his genetic constitution but also by his social relations with other apes. Apes differ in age, sex, size, strength, prowess, etc., and these differences find significant expression in social behavior. The role that an ape plays in the social life of his troop will be determined by the actions and interactions of other apes as well as by his own physiological and morphological properties. In short, the personality—the individuality—of the ape will be determined socially as well as genetically. So significant is the social factor in this respect that a close scientific observer has remarked that "it is hardly an exaggeration to say that a chimpanzee kept in solitude is not a real chimpanzee at all" (Kohler, 1926, p. 293). He goes on to point out that the behavior of the chimpanzee, i.e., his social individuality, is a function of the behavior of other members of his group.

The dependence of chimpanzees, not merely upon the behavior of their fellows but upon an actual social tradition that exists in chimpanzee society in their natural habitat, is vividly set forth by Heini P. Hediger of the Zurich Zoo and University. Why is it, he asks, that so few chimpanzees have been born in zoological gardens: "The number of chimpanzee births lags far behind that, for example, of giraffes and hippopotami" (Hediger, 1961, p. 44). The reason, he says, is that chimpanzees reared in zoos do not know how to perform the act of copulation.

Fully grown chimpanzees are hardly ever caught in Africa, and consequently cannot be exported. The rule is, rather, for babies or barely weaned young, whose parents have been killed, to reach the zoos, where, over the years, they develop into sexually mature specimens. In this manner, that is, through the importation of unknowing young animals, the chain of natural tradition is interrupted. The young that have grown up in isolation literally do not know what to do with their sexual urge upon maturity . . . In many cases, mature pairs, out of ignorance, never get past the stage of sterile masturbation. (*Ibid.*, p. 45)

We have here a truly remarkable situation. Among lower forms of life the act of procreation is performed instinctively. But among the great apes, at least, and in the human species this kind of behavior must be learned. The behavior of a chimpanzee is not merely a function of the behavior of other chimpanzees, as is pointed out by Kohler. It is dependent upon a social tradition which, in a state of nature, is passed down from one individual and generation to another. This tradition is broken when chimpanzees are taken in infancy from their parents and other elders and reared in zoos, either in solitude or among other chimpanzees similarly divorced from the social tradition of mating. Therefore, the mere presence of other chimpanzees is not enough to enable a chimpanzee to perform the act of mating; the actual social tradition of mating must be there also.

We see, then, in this situation that the individual chimpanzee is not only dependent upon the behavior of other chimpanzees to bring out and express his own innate nature, but is dependent upon a social tradition that we can distinguish logically from the continuum of biological parents and children. Indeed, the whole species is dependent upon this tradition; without it they could not mate; they would become extinct.

The individuality of an ape differs significantly from that of a brick. Among bricks there is a maximum of discreteness, a minimum, or near minimum, of particular variation. Among apes, however, discreteness is profoundly qualified on both the biological level and the sociopsychological level. An ape's individuality is a function of—and consequently subordinated to or limited by —his genetic inheritance, the behavior of his fellows, and social tradition. Individuality becomes but a more or less particular expression of two continuums: one biological, the other sociopsychological.

In the species *Homo sapiens,* we note that a man may be considered in three contexts: as a physical object, as a mere animal, and as a human being. Man is, of course, an animal, but he is a unique animal. Only man is capable of originating, determining, and bestowing, freely and arbitrarily, meanings upon things and events in the external world, meanings which cannot be grasped and appreciated with the senses. Holy water is a case in point. Holy water is not the same thing as mere tap water. It is distinguished from ordinary water by a characteristic that is significant to human beings. But this distinguishing characteristic, this meaning or value, cannot be perceived. We call this ability of man to bestow such meanings the ability to symbol. Symboling includes the ability to comprehend nonsensory meanings as well as to originate and bestow them. Symboling, then, consists of traffic in nonsensory meanings. Articulate speech is another example of symboling and is, probably, its most important and characteristic form of expression (see "The Symbol, etc.," in White, 1949a).

All of civilization, or culture, is dependent upon articulate speech. We could not have ideologies, customs, or institutions without articulate speech. Even the human use of tools, as distinguished from tool-using among apes, is, as I have argued elsewhere (White, 1942), dependent upon the ability to symbol. We find, therefore, that man, as a human being, inhabits a world of his own, a unique world, as well as occupying, as a mere animal, the world that apes live in. A human being is subject to the same influences of gravitation, temperature, atmospheric pressure, and humidity as is an ape, and, indeed, a brick. But here the similarity between the physical worlds of an ape and of a human being ends. Culture conditions and qualifies all of man's perceptions— as a human being—of the external world. He does not see the same sun that an ape sees. To the ape the sun is merely an optical and thermal object. But to a human being it is the Sun Father, the

Giver of Life, or a huge mass of thermonuclear transformations. As Ernst Cassirer (1944, pp. 24–25) has put it:

> Man has, as it were, discovered a new method of adapting himself to his environment. Between the receptor system and the effector system . . . we find in man a third link which we may describe as the *symbolic system*. . . . As compared with the other animals man lives not merely in a broader reality [but] in a new dimension of reality. . . . No longer can man confront reality immediately; he cannot see it, as it were, face to face. Physical reality seems to recede in proportion as man's symbolic activity advances. . . . He has so enveloped himself in linguistic forms, in artistic images, in mythical symbols or religious rites that he cannot see or know anything except by the interposition of this artificial medium

We turn now to the question of individuality in the human species. A man is a discrete physical object, as a brick is. As a biological organism he is discrete as an ape is. That is, insofar as he is a complete, autonomous system, his discreteness is complete. But this system, this organism, is not wholly discrete with reference to other organisms; its characteristics have been determined genetically by other organisms, namely, his ancestors. When we turn to the sociopsychological context, we find that it is culture, rather than mere social interaction or a behavioral tradition, that is significant. The individuality of a human being has, therefore, three determinants: first, the discreteness of a complete, autonomous, animate material system; second, the factor of genetic inheritance which tends to limit and constrain individuality by making a child resemble his parents; and, third, the influence of the extrasomatic tradition that we call culture.

Mere social interaction and social tradition are, as we have seen, factors in the determination of individuality among apes. Both these factors are biologically determined. The process of social interaction is determined by such factors as age, sex, size, strength, health, and prowess. Their social tradition—at least in the conspicuous instance of reproduction—is merely a device to facilitate the expression and to guarantee the continuity of a biological process. In the human species, however, both mere social interaction and social tradition are culturally, rather than biologically, determined. It is not, for example, innate biological traits that determine the form of the family or the social traditions of monogamy and polygamy. On the contrary, it is the extrasomatic tradition that we call culture that determines the behavior of the members of the family. And culture is an organization, or system, that behaves in accordance with its own principles and laws. Let us turn, then, to this factor of culture and see how it operates and, specifically, how it affects human individuality.

Culture and man as a human being began simultaneously; both originated in symboling. Symboling produced culture: an organization of beliefs, customs, tools, and techniques. In a relatively short time every society of men acquired a complete, even though simple and crude, culture, and in so doing these men became completely humanized. This culture was transmitted from one generation to another; it flowed down through time indefinitely; it acquired a life of its own, so to speak. It became a process *sui generis,* self-contained, self-determined, and autonomous. To be sure, culture could not exist without human beings. But it is not human beings who determine their culture by desire and design; it is culture that determines the behavior of peoples. The behavior of the culture process, or of cultural systems, is not a function of the human mind; on the contrary, the behavior of peoples is a function of the extrasomatic tradition that is culture (we say peoples, not individuals, because the behavior of an individual is a function of his biological make-up as well as of his culture). The culture process, or cultural systems, behave in accordance with principles and laws of their own. Culture is to be explained culturologically rather than biologically or psychologically. There is, of course, a necessary and intimate relationship between culture as a whole and the human species. If man were not the kind of animal he is, his culture in general would not be what it is. But we cannot explain variations of culture in terms of the biological factor, man. The problems of culture history and the evolution of culture do not require for their solution a consideration of the human organism or species. The culturologist approaches the problems of culture change as if the human race did not exist.

What is the nature of individuality of human beings within the culture process (or cultural system)?[1] They have individuality of a sort, but it is so subordinated to the influence of the extrasomatic tradition of culture as to be almost an individuality without distinctiveness. It is much like the individuality of bricks: each is distinct, but all are made of the same materials, and designed in the same way. Let us consider what takes place in the making of a human being.

An infant of the human species is born into a cultural tradition. At birth, and for some time thereafter, the infant's potential ability to symbol does not reach the point of overt expression. The presymbol child is not a human being from the standpoint of kind of behavior. The infant becomes humanized as he is inducted into his culture through the process of symboling. In this way he acquires all his knowledge and beliefs, his customs and his codes, his attitudes and values, his gods and his hells. A human being is a receptacle into which culture has been poured.

To be sure, the human organism is not a wholly passive object. On the contrary, it is a dynamic system, a thermodynamic system. It does not merely *undergo* experiences; it *does* something about them. Cultural influences impinge upon the human organism;

---

[1] See White, 1949b and 1950, for a previous discussion of this subject.

elements of culture are introduced into it. And the human organism, as a dynamic system, lays hold of them, orders them, corre-
lates and synthesizes them. No two human organisms do this in
precisely the same way, first because no two organisms are exactly
alike, and second because the order in which the organism experiences cultural events is significant. Two organisms, exactly alike
biologically, and reared in the same cultural milieu, could become
different persons as a consequence of the order in which they
underwent certain experiences. Two young women, for example,
could (1) go to college, (2) have a baby, and (3) marry. But
the order in which each one did these things would have a significant effect upon her as an individual.

There is room, then, for individuality among human beings as
a consequence of (1) their respective biological differences, (2)
differences in the temporal order in which events are experienced,
and (3) variations of the cultural factor itself; in a complex cultural system one person might be reared in one subculture, another person in another. But the similarity among human beings
produced by a given culture is striking. Culture exerts a powerful
and overriding influence upon the biological organisms of *Homo
sapiens,* submerging the neurological, anatomical, sensory, glandular, muscular, etc., differences among them to the point of
insignificance.

I remember vividly when, as a youth, I heard for the first time
Negroes speaking French. I had lived in a rural area in the Deep
South where all Negroes spoke, not merely the English language,
but a distinctive dialect of that tongue. Consequently, years later,
I experienced a shock of novelty and of unreflecting surprise
when in the West Indies I heard Negroes speaking French—
much as if I had suddenly heard a lamb roar or a lion bleat.

Language and dialects impose themselves upon the plastic infant organisms that come under their influence. To be sure, no

two persons speak a dialect in exactly the same way. But when one considers the enormous range of biological differences—the endomorphs and exomorphs, the hypothyroid and the hyperthyroid, the prognathous and hypognathous, and all the variations of bony, muscular and neural structure—the similarity of the product, of the dialect spoken, is truly impressive. So impressive, in fact, that one well versed in the geography of dialects can tell where a person was reared by the way he pronounces a few words. And so profoundly does the linguistic tradition influence the organism of a human being that it becomes virtually impossible for him, after he has passed the stage of adolescence, to learn to speak another language without an appreciable accent. It is as if a duck, as a consequence of being reared among turkeys, could no longer quack. The linguistic tradition is like a radio broadcasting station, the organism like the radio that receives the message and reproduces it. If the culture broadcasts Tibetan, the human radios "play" Tibetan; if it broadcasts a Brooklyn dialect of English, the human organism will reproduce that.

As it is with language in particular, so it is with culture as a whole. Just as your culture imposes a language and dialect upon you, so does it equip you with your beliefs, your customs, your attitudes and values. The individual is but a particular re-creation of his culture.

It is ironical that, notwithstanding the fact that this conception of human individuality has been developed and validated by cultural anthropology, we nevertheless find a totally opposed conception, well established in anthropological theory, which we shall now examine. In this respect, however, anthropology does but reflect a more general and popular conception of individuality. The anthropologists who hold this anthropocentric conception of individuality do so not because of anthropological science, but in spite of it. The conception of individuality which we are about to examine is an anthropocentric one.

Thesis. It holds that the human individual is a complete and self-determined whole, and that he is, moreover, a dynamic system, a prime mover, a creator, a first cause. In its extreme form, this conception insists that only individuals are real, that society is merely an aggregation of individuals, and culture but an abstraction.

This exact opposite of a culturological interpretation was espoused by the late Franz Boas, who dominated American anthropology for many years after the turn of the century. "It seems hardly necessary," he wrote, "to consider culture a mystic entity that exists outside the society of its individual carriers and that moves by its own force . . . The forces that bring about the changes are active in the individuals composing the social group, not in the abstract culture" (Boas, 1932a, pp. 245–246).

Comment. Of course culture is not a *mystic* entity, but there is a very real sense in which it has an existence outside the individuals who comprise a society.[2] All material culture—buildings, factories, railroads, etc.—have, of course, their objective being outside individuals. But so also do intellectual and social traditions. The English language, the Ten Commandments, Euclidean geometry, and codes of laws had an existence before any of us was born; they enter our minds from the outside; and they will continue to exist after we are gone. It is self-evident that culture could not "move" were it not for human beings, who make the

[2] ". . . collective ways of acting and thinking [i.e., culture] have a reality outside the individuals who, at every moment of time, conform to it. These ways of thinking and acting exist in their own right. The individual finds them completely formed, and he cannot evade or change them. He is therefore obliged to reckon with them."—Emile Durkheim, *The Rules of Sociological Method,* preface to the second edition, p. lvi.

culture process possible. But from the standpoint of a scientific explanation of the process of culture change, we do not need to take individuals into account; indeed we may disregard human beings entirely. We do not need, for example, to concern ourselves with human beings when we deal with such matters as the diffusion of the use of tobacco throughout the world after the discoveries of Columbus, or the evolution of currency, or the constitutional, parliamentary form of government. People could not solve problems in algebra or compose symphonies were it not for respiration. But we do not need to take respiration into account in a scientific explanation of such behavior.

Thesis. The anthropocentric, anticulturological point of view is frequently expressed in the assertion that it is people, not culture, who do things. "But culture does not 'work,' 'move,' 'change,' but is worked, is moved, is changed. It is people who do things . . ." says Robert S. Lynd. He goes on to say, "The culture does not enamel its fingernails, or vote, or believe in capitalism, but people do" (Lynd, 1939, pp. 38, 39). And Edward Sapir, a prominent student of Boas, declares that "it is always the individual that really thinks and acts and dreams and revolts" (Sapir, 1917, p. 442).

Comment. Of course it is people who enamel their fingernails; as a matter of fact, culture *has* no fingernails. And thinking and dreaming are processes that have their loci in individual biological organisms. But the intent and purpose of Lynd and Sapir are not to utter these commonplaces, but to express a philosophy of behavior. From the standpoint of science, the question is not *who* does this or that, people or culture, but *why* do people do the things they do. And the reason why one people enamels their fingernails while another blackens their teeth, or tatoos their faces, is because they are responding to different extrasomatic cultural traditions. As for thinking and dreaming, these are processes which, by definition, take place within a biological organism. But *what* the individual thinks and dreams is determined by his culture: a Hottentot does not think or dream as does a Frenchman.

Thesis. Some outstanding and influential anthropologists have conceived of the individual as a First Cause. "The individual, with his physiological needs and psychological processes," said Malinowski, "is the ultimate source . . . of all tradition, activities, and organized behavior" (Malinowski, 1939, p. 962). Similarly, Goldenweiser "places the individual both at the beginning and at the end of the social process. Human society," he says, "was built out of the needs, proclivities and achievements of individuals . . ." (Goldenweiser, 1935, p. 75). Thus, to these students, it is the individual who creates culture. "It is the individual," said Ralph Linton, "who is responsible, in the last analysis, for all additions to culture. Every new idea must originate with some person" (Linton, 1938, p. 248). To Edward Sapir, "Any culture element . . . has radiated out, at last analysis [*last analysis* suggests that there is nothing more to be said], from a single individual" (Sapir, 1916, p. 43). "The inventive process resides in individual organisms," says Clark Wissler; "it is a function of the individual organism" (Wissler, 1927, p. 87). Ruth Benedict, too, has offered an "in the last analysis" pronouncement: "No civilization has in it any element which in the last analysis is not the contribution of an individual. Where else could any trait come from except from the behavior of a man or a woman or a child?" (Benedict, 1934, p. 253).

Let me hasten to point out that this conception of the individual's role in the culture process is not confined to anthropology. William James expressed it long ago in his essay, "Great Men, Great Thoughts and the Environment." The genesis of great ideas, and inventions is, he says, "sudden and, as it were, spontaneous . . . [a] conception . . . is a spontaneous variation in the strictest sense of the term . . . [inventions such as the yardstick, the balance, the chronometer] and all other institutions were flashes of genius in an individual head, *of which the outer environment showed no sign"* (James, 1880, pp. 456–458; emphasis mine).

Comment. It all seems so simple and so obvious: where else could an invention occur, a new culture trait originate, except in the mind of "a man or a woman or a child"? Simple and obvious, perhaps, but so anthropocentric. How could a human individual, divorced from culture, invent or originate anything cultural? In the first place, as we have already seen, an individual divorced from a cultural milieu would not be a human being; he would be a mere hominid. Furthermore, without cultural material to work with, the individual could do nothing of cultural significance. An invention—a new conception, a new tool, or a new institution —is a novel permutation or combination of culture traits effected within the interactive process that is a cultural tradition. An invention, the steam engine, for example, is a synthesis of already existing cultural elements—the technique of making fire, a knowledge of metallurgy, cylinders, pistons, cranks, and wheels. The steam engine has a genealogy. It is the culturological descendant of many elements of culture, each of which in turn can be traced back in time, sometimes to remotest antiquity, as in the case of firemaking. The invention of the steam engine was not a single event, achieved by a single individual, but a sociotechnological process involving the labor of scores of individuals in several nations over a period of centuries. The fact that dozens of inventions and discoveries have been made simultaneously by two, sometimes several, persons working quite independently of one another is a significant indication of cultural determination rather than of individual initiative or genius. When the interactive culture process reaches a certain point of development, an invention or discovery becomes not only possible but inevitable (White, 1949a, pp. 168–170, 203–211; see also Ogburn and Thomas, 1922, pp. 83–98).

To get back to a point that we have touched upon before, if one means merely that neurological processes of individual organisms are essential to the synthesis of elements in the extrasomatic cultural tradition (Kroeber and Kluckhohn [1952, p. 172] say that "each new or changed value takes its concrete origin [as do all aspects of culture] in the psychological processes of some particular individual"), then of course we must grant that this is true. Neurological processes are essential to the social process of culture change and invention, and by definition, they are functions of the biological organism, not of the social organism, or body politic. But to say, as William James did, or to imply as others have done, that the individual is the creator, the originator, the prime mover is a gross distortion, an example of crass anthropocentrism. To say, as William James did, that a man invented something because he was a genius is one thing; to say that the individual was the locus within which a significant synthesis of cultural elements took place is quite another. To be sure, one human organism may be a better neurological locus than another, but we have no way of measuring the innate inventive capacity of a nervous system directly. To say that one who has made a great invention is a genius, i.e., has superior innate ability, is to make a neurological inference from culturological evidence. And to account for a great invention in terms of such genius is to explain the known facts of culturology by the unknown facts of neurology—which is not very good science.

Thesis. With regard to the question of culture change in general, many anthropologists have held that here also, as in the case of invention, the individual effects the changes. "When patterns [of culture,] change," says the British social anthropologist Raymond Firth, "it is individuals in the last resort [*sic*] who change them" (Firth, 1951, p. 85). Indeed, they conceive of individuals as standing outside their culture and, by their own actions, changing it—in the same way that man can, and has, changed natural environments by deforestation, irrigation or drainage, exterminating vast herds of bison, and bringing prairies under cultivation. Thus, Franz Boas not only distinguishes between the culture that he lives in and his ideals but tells us that the culture ran counter to his ideals (Boas, 1938, p. 204).

Exceptionally able individuals are more likely to change their cultures than are mediocre ones, according to this thesis. In small groups of primitive peoples, says Lowie (1948, p. 84), "a few resolute spirits can easily impose an innovation." "Dominant personalities" effect changes in art, science, philosophy, and literature, according to Goldenweiser (1922, p. 26). To turn to nonanthropologists, William James asserts that culture change "is due to the accumulated influences of individuals, of their examples, their initiatives, and their decisions" (1880, p. 242). And Arnold Toynbee, according to Roger J. Williams, "makes clear the crucial importance of individual creative souls in any society and indicates that the breakdown of any civilization is primarily traced to the failure in the creative power of the individuals who should be like leaven in the lump" (Williams, 1950, p. 54).

But it is not only the "dominant personalities," the "resolute spirits," and the "creative souls" who change the course and content of culture, according to this view. The unstable, the maladjusted, and the nonconformists also produce changes. William James (1880, pp. 456–457) says that a conception "flashes out of one brain, and no other, because the instability of that brain is such as to tip and upset itself in just that particular direction."

It is the dissatisfied and the dissident who bring about culture change, according to anthropologist Homer Barnett. "Finally," he says (Barnett, 1941, p. 171), "to put the finger on *the ultimate source of all cultural change* [emphasis mine], it may be bold but it is not unreasonable to suggest some kind of personal conflict as the primary motivation for invention. In other words, there are good reasons for believing that the inventor is such because he feels, rather acutely and personally, a dissatisfaction with the customary and accepted ways of doing things. This is demonstrably true of the social inventor, the 'liberal,' and it is no less reasonable to posit some motor or affective thwartings at the source of technological inventions." Barnett excepts "the professional inventor of our nineteenth and twentieth century civilization" from this generalization. The professional inventor "does not really alter the picture," says Barnett; he merely "adds to it." And, finally, Boas (1938, p. 202) believed that culture changes were brought about, "in part at least," by "non-conformists."

Comment. Here is another simple and easy explanation of the process of culture change: if an individual doesn't like his culture he changes it. If he is a "dominant personality" or a "creative soul" he modifies or improves his culture as a sculptor shapes a piece of marble under his hands. Or, if the individual is maladjusted, if he suffers from "personal conflicts," or is simply a "nonconformist," he sets about to change the culture and make it more to his liking. Again we find the simple, easy, anthropocentric explanation. As a matter of fact, it reminds one of the deistic explanations in Genesis. To paraphrase this Book, we might speak as follows: "And Man surveyed the culture he had made and was not pleased with his handwork. He therefore said, 'Let there be change,' and there was change." Anthropomorphism is simply deism reduced to human dimensions.

As for Boas' culture running counter to his ideals, he obviously had no understanding of the origin and substance of his ideals. He believed that they originated within himself, not only independently of his culture but in opposition to it. He did not realize that he was born without ideals and that had he grown up outside a cultural tradition he would have had no more ideals than a gorilla has,[3] or that if he had been reared in a Tibetan household he would have acquired different ideals. Boas' ideals were expressions of his culture just as his language, beliefs, and table manners were. The opposition between his ideals and his culture was due to the fact that a complex culture like our own is not homogeneous and wholly self-consistent. On the contrary, it is divided against itself at many points. Boas' personal conflict was also a conflict within his culture.

I shall not criticize in detail the Great Man theory of history here inasmuch as I have done so at some length elsewhere (e.g., in "Ikhnaton: The Great Man vs. the Culture Process," "Genius: Its Causes and Incidence," "Cultural Determinants of Mind," etc., in *The Science of Culture*.) The culturologist does not maintain that the individuality of human beings is wholly irrelevant to a scientific explanation of the process of culture change. Human organisms are the medium through which the culture process expresses itself; they are the instruments by means of which the culture process effects its changes and produces its results. Since no two human organisms are alike in neurological, glandular, muscular, sensory, et cetera, structure and organization, the be-

---

[3] The individual "is nothing, at best an idiot; only through spoken intercourse in society does he become conscious of thought, is his nature realized. The thought of society, social thought, is the primary result and the thought of the individual is won by later analysis from it."—Adolph Bastian, *Die Vorgeschichte der Ethnologie*, p. 79 (1890). These words were quoted by Ludwig Gumplowicz in *The Outlines of Sociology*, p. 45 (Philadelphia, 1899), who commented: "These words are golden and we shall accept them as the motto of sociology."

havior of the culture process is conditioned by biological variations. No two people speak the English language exactly alike, and the particular and unique biological characteristics of the organism which is the head of a state affect the behavior of that sociocultural system. But we might note four significant facts in this connection.

In the first place, the Great Man, as a head of state, is a person who has been selected by a sociocultural system, i.e., the nation, and placed in that position. Hitler was placed at the head of the German nation by the nation itself, operating, of course, as all modern nations do, through the groupings of powerful political, economic, industrial, and military forces; it was not the little rabble rouser who captured the German nation singlehanded. A person becomes a Great Man in history when and because he is placed, by forces and agencies outside himself, in the midst of powerful cultural processes. Had not the Civil War come along and swept Ulysses S. Grant into its vortex, he would have remained an obscure and insignificant clerk in his father's leather store in Galena, Illinois.

Second, anyone who is selected by a sociocultural system and placed in a position of political power is, and must be, a person who is susceptible to social influence and the more the better; a person wholly impervious to social influence would not only *not* be an asset, but a serious liability.

Third, to be a significant factor in the process of sociocultural change, a man does not need to be a "dominant personality" or a "creative soul." In fact, he may be a most mediocre person. If we grant, as we do, that the course of the Russian Revolution in 1917 was appreciably, or even profoundly, affected by the unique and innate traits of Nicolai Lenin, then we must also admit that a stupid and nondescript switchman could have had a like influence upon the course of events if he had forgotten to close a switch, thus wrecking the train which was bringing Lenin to Petrograd, and killing Lenin. Indeed, the course of history can be significantly affected by nonhuman beings. It was a goose that saved Rome, and Mrs. O'Leary's cow that set the city of Chicago on fire.

Finally, the head of a great state has actually less individuality and freedom of action than an ordinary citizen in lesser walks of life. The President of the United States today enjoys less freedom of action and has fewer choices of alternatives than I. In his public and his personal life he is under constant surveillance and control by Secret Service men, newspaper reporters, and the general public. He is not as free to do as he pleases, to go where he wishes, as I am. I could go to a Florida resort for a long weekend with a spouse not my own with much greater anonymity and with fewer risks than could the President. With regard to decisions, I have greater freedom and control. The President's decisions can hardly be called his own at all. He is briefed by his aides, counselled by his advisors, pushed and pulled by countless political factions and economic interests. His "decisions," therefore, are but the expression of an integration and synthesis of literally thousands of social and political processes which belong to the body politic. The chief executive is but the meter which measures them and the mouthpiece which gives them expression. And I compose my own lectures; no one writes them for me.

To test our theory, let us imagine the President making a decision of his own. Suppose that he should, upon arising some morning, decide and declare that the United States should immediately and forthwith embark upon a program of absolute and complete unilateral disarmament. This would come about as close to being a decision of his own as would be possible. What would be the consequences? It is likely that the President would be quietly and unostentatiously removed to some secluded sanitarium where he could do no harm. (In certain "nondemocratic" countries a head of state who took similar independent action might well be executed.) Our nation could not tolerate such an individual. The sudden termination of our vast munitions industries and the collapse of our economic system could not be permitted to take place.

But I am not a wholly free, discrete, autonomous individual, either. I must work within the limits of the structure and behavior of my University; and I must behave within the boundaries of the folkways and mores of my residential community. I do indeed compose my own lectures, but I only synthesize materials bestowed upon me by a scientific tradition. I can decide, but again within the limits of the Department of Anthropology, whether I will give a course on ethnological theory or primitive economics. But I cannot tell my students that man was created in the year 4004 B.C., or that the earth is flat and motionless. In my private life—and I have much more life that is private than does the President—I have much freedom to come and go as I please and to do what I wish, but always as a consequence of the values and goals that my culture has given me.

As a good scientist—as good, at least, as I *can* be—I am loath to discuss matters about which I know little. But, upon the basis of rather meager knowledge, I am inclined to think that the individual who has enjoyed the greatest amount of freedom of choice, decision, and action in our society in the twentieth century has been the hobo. Actually, I am not sure that this species has not now become extinct. But as a youth I saw many, met some, and acquired some reliable information about them. Nels Anderson, the author of an informative and illuminating monograph entitled *The Hobo,* was a fellow student of mine at The University of Chicago in the 1920s.

The American hobo, as his image appears to me, was probably

the most individualistic individual that our society ever produced, the freest, the most discrete—the antithesis of the organization man—the most autonomous. If I have more freedom than the President of the United States, greater range of alternatives, choices, and action, then the hobo had much greater freedom and individuality than I. He was as close an approximation as it is possible to achieve to the ideal held by anthropologists like Franz Boas, philosophers like William James, and historians like Arnold Toynbee of the discrete, autonomous individual. Yet the hobo did not change his culture; he was the victim, a casualty, of it. A hobo is a product of a particular kind of culture; there were no hobos among the Eskimos or the Zuñi Pueblo Indians.

Emphasis upon individuality and individualism occurs at still another point in American anthropology. Franz Boas was "of Jewish extraction." The exasperating phenomenon of anti-Semitism was of much concern to Boas not only in his formative years, as Kluckhohn and Prufer have pointed out, but throughout his entire life. Many of his more prominent students were Jewish, also.[4] As members of a minority group, many anthropologists of the Boas school were much concerned with the question of racial conflicts. *The Mind of Primitive Man* (1911; revised 1938), undoubtedly Boas' best known book, has race as its central thesis, and *Race and Democratic Society,* a volume of essays and lectures by Boas, published posthumously (1945), is much concerned with race problems.

In his discussion of race, Boas exalts the individual and minimizes the significance of race. "Many hereditary characteristics," he says, "are not racial in character, but must be assigned to family lines . . . any generalized characterization of a race must be

---

[4] John Sholtz, writing in *Reflex: A Jewish Magazine,* Vol. 6 (1935) comments upon "the disproportionate position held by Jewish scientists" in the field of anthropology in the United States.

misleading" (Boas, 1945, p. 26). And "if it can be shown that each family line differs in its hereditary traits from all others then it would be impossible to speak . . . of hereditary traits common to the whole group [i.e., race]" (*ibid.*, p. 31). As a matter of fact, Boas comes rather close to making race disappear. "When we talk about the characteristics of a race as a whole," he says, "we are dealing with an abstraction which has no existence in nature" (*ibid.*, p. 70). If it could be shown that races do not really exist, then a logical basis for racial prejudice and discrimination would be removed. Unfortunately, prejudice does not need a logical basis in order to flourish.

Boas made a desperate effort to subordinate race to the individual. He does not go so far as to say that a race is "nothing but" a plural number of individuals. But he does quote "the eminent German anthropologist, Eugen Fischer, [who] went so far as to say—before the Hitler revolution—that every individual is a racial unit" (*ibid.*, p. 44). And again and again he declares that members of minority groups "have the right to be treated as individuals, not as members of a class [race]" (*ibid.*, p. 79). "According to our modern theoretical standards," he says, "we maintain that justice should be given to the individual, that it should not be meted out to him as to a representative of his class [race]" (*ibid.*, p. 79).

Other members of the Boas school were ardent individualists also. In his essay, "Why I am not a Marxist," Goldenweiser gave, as one of the reasons at least, that he was an arch individualist (Goldenweiser, 1935, p. 75). And, as we have already seen, Sapir regarded the individual as a prime mover, the creator and determinant of the culture process.

This emphasis upon the individual in American anthropology had much to do, in my opinion, with the origin and development of the Personality and Culture Movement that was so popular during the 1930s. As early as 1923, according to Ruth Benedict, a close associate and colleague of Boas, Professor Boas believed that his campaign to establish diffusionism in the place of evolutionism had been successful, and that "as he saw it, anthropology should spend its energies answering these questions of the interplay of the individual and culture" (Benedict, 1943, p. 61). In 1930 Boas stressed the need for "a penetrating study of the individual under the stress of the culture in which he lives" as opposed to studies of historical reconstruction (Boas, 1930, p 269). In his presidential address to the American Association for the Advancement of Science in 1932, he observed that

problems of the relation of the individual to his culture . . . have received too little attention. The standardized anthropological data that inform us of customary behavior, give no clue to the reaction to his culture, nor to an understanding of *his influence upon it*. Still, *here lie the sources of a true interpretation of human behavior*. It seems a vain effort to search for sociological [not cultural, or culturological] laws disregarding what should be called social psychology, namely, the reaction of the individual to culture. *They can be no more than empty formulas that can be imbued with life only by taking account of individual behavior in cultural settings*. (Boas, 1932b, pp. 257–259; emphasis mine.)

And in one of the last articles he ever wrote, published posthumously, Boas could say that "one of the characteristic traits of modern anthropology" *was* "the emphasis laid on the relation between individual and culture . . ." (Boas, 1943, pp. 313–314).

Thus we find in the social philosophy and social science of American scholars a coherent philosophy of reality: of society, culture, and the individual. In this philosophy, the individual is not only first and foremost, but, in extreme cases, the only reality. "Every society," says Ralph Linton, "is, in the last analysis, a group of individuals" (Linton, 1945, p. xiv). But a society is merely a "conceptual construct" (Kluckhohn and Kelly, 1945, p. 80), and culture but an imperceptible abstraction (see White, 1959a, pp. 227–228). If culture is imperceptible, does it really exist? One anthropologist has summarized contemporary thinking on this point by declaring that "culture has no ontological reality" (Spiro, 1951, p. 24). In its extreme form, this philosophy holds that only the individual is real, a belief that is more frequently implicit than explicit. But sometimes it is asserted in a forthright manner. We recall a distinguished German sociologist, Georg Simmel (1858–1918), who, after surveying phenomena ordinarily called social and cultural, declared that "it is certain that in the last analysis only individuals exist" (Simmel, 1898, p. 665; see also Vierkandt, 1934, p. 61).

We hold that this philosophic view of man and culture is but a simple, and rather crude form of anthropocentrism. Its concepts rest directly upon, and immediately express, percepts. One can see an individual; therefore he exists. One cannot see culture; therefore it "has no ontological reality." This view is made explicit by one of the anthropologists in Kluckhohn and Kelly's imaginary symposium (1945, p. 81). He expresses his dissatisfaction with the concept of culture, saying, "I maintain that we would get further if we stuck to human interaction with other humans and with the natural environment. You can see those things, but has any of you ever seen 'culture'?"

This self-imposed limitation upon the intellect is pathetic. One might argue that no one ever saw a vegetable, but only carrots, onions, etc.; or that no one can see a university, but only this building and that. "Vegetable" is the name of a class of phenomena, and members of this class can certainly be seen. "University" is the name of interrelated, real, observable things and events. To limit the exercise of the intellect to optical perception is to make science utterly impossible. No one ever saw the solar system with his eyes, but only the sun and planets. But the scientist "sees" with the eyes of his mind, not merely with his retina, optic nerve, and so on. The naïveté of the anthropomorphic conception of culture is made apparent by imagining the observer equipped with a different kind of eyes. Suppose he had eyes that could clearly distinguish the cells of the human body. Then he would declare that "in the last analysis"—he would, of course, have to say, "in the last analysis"—only cells are real; a human being is merely an anatomical construct. If he had eyes that could distinguish molecules or atoms, then they would, in the last analysis, be the only realities. And if he had the ultimate in microscopic vision, he would find that only electrons, protons, mesons, etc., are real, that even atoms are but logical constructs. And, at the other end of the spectrum, if our observer had macroscopic vision, perhaps he could not see individuals at all but only crowds; only forests, no trees. Are we to tolerate a philosophy in which the nature of reality is determined by variations of optical perception?

To be sure, science must postulate a real world external to and independent of the observer.[5] And our knowledge and understanding of this external world must arise out of and depend upon our sensory perceptions of it (see Einstein, 1936, pp. 350 *et passim*). But to think of perceptions as the starting point of knowledge and understanding is one thing; to limit conceptions to the narrow boundaries of perception is quite another matter. And it is conceptions that count in science. One might argue that one cannot see a football team but only the individual players. But then he would be obliged to say, if he were consistent, that he could not see a quarterback at all, because a quarterback is an individual in a network of relationships and

[5] "The belief in an external world independent of the perceiving subject is the basis of all natural science."—Einstein, *The World As I See It*, p. 60.

one cannot see "a network of social relationships." Similarly, one could not see a slave because he could perceive only the biological object, not the institution of slavery. Corn and cotton are not commodities per se; they become commodities only when they are significant in certain contexts. These contexts are not observable via the retina and optic nerve; they are conceptions. And conceptions are the building blocks of science. One cannot well imagine a more effective way to sabotage scientific endeavor than to limit it to sensory perceptions.

To return now to the three major concepts of the science of man and his work: the individual, society, and culture. The individual is, first of all a physical object. It is discrete, it has weight and dimensions. And, although it resembles other members of its class, it can be distinguished from them by its possession of more or less particular characteristics. Second, an individual is a biological organism. A biological organism is, of course, still a physical object, but it is one whose individuality has been determined in part by other biological organisms, namely, its ancestors. As a biological organism, an individual is an expression of a network of relationships as well as being a discrete and autonomous system. Third, a member of the species *Homo sapiens* would, as a mere animal, be a member of a society if there were in actuality any such thing as human men apart from culture. Man cannot, therefore, be merely a *social* animal, but only a socio-*cultural* animal which is not a mere animal but a human being (see White, 1959b). Finally, a human individual is a member of a sociocultural system. As such, his individuality is determined by the extrasomatic cultural tradition in which he lives as well as by his own biological equipment. And, as we have seen, the cultural tradition completely overrides the biological basis of behavior, at least as far as groups, peoples, are concerned. And even in the case of individual organisms, one's religion, values, customs, and beliefs are determined by one's culture rather than by one's nerves, glands, muscles, and sense organs.

To return to Simmel's dictum that only individuals are real, we must ask what is the nature of the reality, or of the several realities, of the human individual. We have just reviewed the three levels of reality: physical, biological, and sociocultural. Every individual is, by definition, a member of a class. As a physical object, a human individual is both discrete and independent. As a biological organism he is discrete in one sense but is a point in a network of genetic relationships in another. And as a human being, the individual is primarily and predominantly an expression of a particular synthesis of cultural elements; his individuality is even less as a human being than as a biological organism. As Karl Marx observed many years ago: "But the essence of man is no abstraction inherent in each separate individual. In its reality it is in the ensemble of social relations" (Sixth of the Theses on Feurbach).

What then are we to say about society and culture whose reality has often been questioned or denied, as compared with the attribution of reality to individuals? As soon as we disabuse ourselves of the notion that only those things that we can see are real, and after we have distinguished between seeing with retinas and optic nerves and seeing with the mind's eye—the eye of science—we shall have no trouble.

"Society" is the name that we give to a plural number of individuals who interact with one another. A society is a network of relationships among individuals. The relationships *and the network* are as real as the individuals. It is nonsense to say that the earth is real and the sun is real, because we can see them, but that the relationship between them is not real because we cannot see it. "Relationship" is a concept in the mind of the scientist, but the concept corresponds to an observable reality in the external world. It is the same with "fox," "gene," or "electron." These are both concepts and things or events in the external world.

And so it is with culture. "Culture" is the name that anthropological science has given to a class of phenomena. These phenomena are as real as stars or atoms and, like stars and atoms, they exist in the external world, locatable in terrestrial time and space. "Culture" is the name of things and events, dependent upon man's unique ability to symbol, considered in an extrasomatic context (White, 1959a, p. 234). Things and events dependent upon symboling include language, beliefs, customs, tools, utensils, works and forms of art, and so on. A thing or event is said to be in a somatic context when it is considered in terms of its relationship to the human organism. It is in an extrasomatic context when it is considered, not in terms of its relationship to the human organism, but in terms of itself and in terms of its relationship to other things and events. Thus when we consider the mother-in-law taboo in a somatic context we are concerned with the conceptions, attitudes, and acts of the persons concerned. When we consider it in an extrasomatic context we are concerned with the relationship of this taboo to other customs, such as place of residence after marriage, the division of labor between the sexes, customs of inheritance, and so on. Things dependent upon symboling considered in a somatic context we call "human behavior"; when considered in an extrasomatic context we call them "culture" (see White, 1959a, p. 231).

To say that society and culture are not real because one cannot "see" them is nonsense, scientific nonsense. One might as well say that the solar system or the Supreme Court is not real. Or, as we have said before, one might as reasonably argue that the individual is not real, that only cells, molecules, atoms, or sub-atomic particles are real. Anthropomorphism, anthropocentrism—the exaltation of the individual human being—as a philosophic tradition is old and well established in the cultures of the world. It is not only prescientific; it is antiscientific. It is one of the greatest, if not the greatest, obstacle to the achievement of the sciences of man, culture, and society that I can think of. But, in competition with the nonanthropomorphic conceptions of science, it will eventually be rendered obsolete and will be liquidated.

Literature Cited

Anderson, Nels
    1923 *The Hobo: The Sociology of the Homeless Man.* Chicago, The
          University of Chicago Press.
Barnett, Homer G.
    1941 "Personal Conflicts and Cultural Changes," In: *Social Forces,* Vol.
          20, pp. 160–171.
Benedict, Ruth
    1934 *Patterns of Culture.* Boston, Houghton Mifflin Company.
    1943 "Obituary of Franz Boas," In: *Science,* Vol. 97, pp. 60–62.
Boas, Franz
    1930 "Some Problems in the Methodology of the Social Sciences," In:
          The New Social Science. Leonard D. White, ed. Chicago, The University of Chicago Press.
    1932 a *Anthropology and Modern Life.* Revised edition. New York,
          W. W. Norton & Company, Inc.
    1932 b "The Aims of Anthropoligcal Research," In: *Science,* Vol. 76, pp.
          605–613. Reprinted in F. Boas, *Race, Language and Culture.* New
          York, Macmillan Company, 1940.
    1938 "An Anthropologist's Credo," In: *The Nation,* Vol. 147, pp. 201–
          204.
    1943 "Recent Anthropology," In: *Science,* Vol. 98, pp. 311–314.
    1945 *Race and Democratic Society.* New York, J. J. Augustin, Inc.

Cassirer, Ernest
   1944   *An Essay on Man.* New Haven, Connecticut, Yale University Press.

Durkheim, Emile
   1938   *The Rules of Sociological Method.* 8th ed. Chicago, University of
          Chicago Press.

Einstein, Albert
   1934   *The World As I See It.* New York, Covici, Friede, Inc.
   1936   "Physics and Reality," In: *Journal of the Franklin Institute,* Vol.
          221, pp. 313–347 in German; pp. 349–382 in English.

Firth, Raymond
   1951   *Elements of Social Organization.* London, C. A. Watts & Company,
          Ltd.

Goldenweiser, Alexander
   1922   *Early Civilization.* New York, Alfred A. Knopf, Inc.
   1935   "Why I am not a Marxist," In: *The Modern Monthly,* Vol. 9, pp.
          71–76.

Hediger, Heini P.
   1961   "The Evolution of Territorial Behavior," In: *The Social Life of
          Early Man.* Sherwood L. Washburn, ed. Chicago, Aldine Publish-
          ing Company.

James, William
   1880   "Great Men, Great Thoughts and Their Environment," In: *At-
          lantic Monthly,* Vol. 46, pp. 441–459.

Kluckhohn, Clyde, and William H. Kelly
   1945   "The Concept of Culture," In: *The Science of Man in the World
          Crisis.* Ralph Linton, ed., pp. 78–106. New York, Columbia Uni-
          versity Press.

Kluckhohn, Clyde, and Olaf Prufer
   1959   "Influence during the Formative Years," In: *The Anthropology of
          Franz Boas.* Walter Goldschmidt, ed. Memoir 89, American An-
          thropological Association, pp. 4–28.

Kohler, Wolfgang
   1926   *The Mentality of Apes.* New York, Harcourt, Brace and Company,
          Inc.

Kroeber, A. L., and Clyde Kluckhohn
   1952   *Culture, A Critical Review of Concepts and Definitions.* Papers of
          the Peabody Museum of American Archaeology and Ethnology,
          Vol. 47 (1), Cambridge, Massachusetts.

Linton, Ralph
   1938 "The Present Status of Anthropology," In: *Science,* Vol. 87, pp. 241–248.
   1945 *The Cultural Background of Personality.* New York, D. Appleton-Century Company, Inc.

Lowie, Robert H.
   1947 *Franz Boas, 1858–1942. Biographical Memoirs, National Academy of Science,* Vol. 24, pp. 303–322.
   1948 *Social Organization.* New York. Rinehart & Company, Inc.

Lynd, Robert S.
   1939 *Knowledge for What?* Princeton, Princeton University Press.

Malinowski, Bronislaw
   1939 "The Group and the Individual in Functional Analysis," In: *American Journal of Sociology,* Vol. 44, pp. 938–964.

Ogburn, William F., and Dorothy Thomas
   1922 "Are Inventions Inevitable?" In: *Political Science Quarterly,* Vol. 37, pp. 83–98.

Sapir, Edward
   1916 *Time Perspective in Aboriginal Culture, A Study of Method.* Memoir 90, Canada Department of Mines, Ottawa.
   1917 "Do We Need a Superorganic?" In: *American Anthropologist,* Vol. 19, pp. 441–447.

Simmel, Georg
   1898 "The Persistence of Social Groups," In: *American Journal of Sociology,* Vol. 3, pp. 662–698.

Spiro, Melford E.
   1951 "Culture and Personality," In: *Psychiatry,* Vol. 14, pp. 19–46.

Vierkandt, Alfred Ferdinand
   1934 "Georg Simmel, 1858–1918," In: *Encyclopedia of the Social Sciences,* Vol. 14, p. 61.

White, Leslie A.
   1942 "On the Use of Tools by Primates," In: *Journal of Comparative Psychology,* Vol. 34, pp. 369–374. Reprinted in *Man in Contemporary Society,* New York, Columbia University Press, Vol. I, pp. 58–64, 1955; in *Readings in Introductory Anthropology,* Elman R. Service, ed., Ann Arbor, Michigan, Edwards Bros., Inc., 1956; and in *Reprint Series in the Social Sciences,* Bobbs-Merrill Company, Inc., 1962.
   1949 a *The Science of Culture.* New York: Farrar, Straus & Company; reissued in paperback by The Grove Press, 1958.

1949 b "The Individual and the Culture Process," In: *Journal of American College of Dentists,* Vol. 16 (1), pp. 3–10.

1950   "The Individual and the Culture Process," In: *Centennial,* American Association for the Advancement of Science, Washington, D.C. (This is an entirely differently worded equivalent of 1949 b.)

1959 a "The Concept of Culture," In: *American Anthropologist,* Vol. 61, pp. 227–251. Reprinted in Portuguese translation in *Educaçao e Ciéncias Sociais,* Vol. 8, No. 14, pp. 17–56, 1960, in Rio de Janeiro, Brazil; in *Culture and the Evolution of Man,* M. F. Ashley Montagu, ed., pp. 38–64, New York, Oxford University Press, 1962; and in *Reprint Series in the Social Sciences,* Bobbs-Merrill Company, Inc., 1962.

1959 b "Man, Culture and Human Beings," In: *Michigan Alumnus Quarterly Review,* Vol. 66, pp. 1–6.

1962   "Symboling: A Kind of Behavior," In: *The Journal of Psychology,* Vol. 53, pp. 311–317.

Williams, Roger J.

1950   "The Human Frontier," In: *Centennial,* American Association for the Advancement of Science, Washington, D.C.

Wissler, Clark

1927   "Recent Developments in Anthropology," In: *Recent Developments in the Social Sciences,* E. C. Hayes, ed., Philadelphia, J. B. Lippincott Company.

◇◇◇

Individualism—or Something
A Plea for Verbal Pluralism

CLARENCE E. AYRES

SOME YEARS AGO, when Hitler was at his apogee, a high Nazi officer was said to have remarked that whenever he heard the word "culture" he loosened his pistol in its holster. With some difference of voltage and implementation, that is how I have long felt about the word "individual." It would be a wild exaggeration to say that those who use it are either fools or scoundrels. As a matter of fact we all use it constantly, just as we all use the first-person-singular pronoun, notwithstanding John Dewey's dictum that it is the most misleading word in the language. As used in ordinary conversation both words are harmless enough. Each of us is in fact a separate and unique specimen of *Homo sapiens,* unique in the same sense that every grain of sand is unique. No other is that one. But these words, harmless enough in common usage, contain a high explosive which one false move may detonate. Descartes exploded the first-person-singular pronoun into a metaphysics of Ultimate Reality, and people are blowing their heads off with "individualism" all the time.

A striking example of this was provided only a few years ago by a Very Eminent Personage. As circumstances dictated, he used to appear before the nation on television every now and then; and his favorite homiletical gambit was the solemn pronouncement that the difference between this country and certain other countries lies in the fact that, whereas in those countries the individual exists for the state, in this country the state exists for the individual. I used to sit in fascination, watching his well-meaning, solemn face and wondering what in the world he could possibly imagine he was saying. How does one conceive "the state" as an entity distinct and separate from the individuals who (one would suppose) *are* it? Certainly there are very great differences between one state and another, just as there are between one individual and another. But the former very definitely correspond to the latter, or vice versa. Surely no one supposes that the Soviet Union consists of two hundred million Americans dominated by a monolithic party dictatorship! Do "I" "exist for" the cells which compose "my" body and which will certainly die when "I" die, or do they "exist for" "me"?

The meaninglessness of the concept "individual" is a very old story. But the concept is kept alive by the language, and so the story has to be perennially retold. It has never been told better than by Charles Horton Cooley more than half a century ago in the opening pages of *Human Nature and the Social Order.* "A separate individual," Cooley wrote in one of the most frequently quoted sentences in the literature of modern social science, "is an abstraction unknown to experience"; and he continued:

and so likewise is society when regarded as something apart from individuals. The real thing is human life, which may be considered either in an individual aspect or in a social, that is to say general, aspect; but is always, as a matter of fact, both individual and general. In other words "society" and "individuals" do not denote separate phenomena, but are simply collective and distributive aspects of the same thing, the relations between them being like that between other expressions one of which denotes a group as a whole and the other the members of the group, such as an army and the soldiers, the class and the students, and so on.

One might ask a general whether an army exists for the soldiers, or whether the soldiers exist for the army, and what does "for" mean in such a sentence?

The trouble is that "individual" is a stop-thought word. It numbs the mind, so that once it has been uttered, inquiry stops. All seems to have been said that needs to be said. But that is never the case. In fact, nothing has been said. Everyone knows that there are very great differences between the Soviet Union and the United States, differences which affect every aspect of life. Party dictatorship is as different from the national state which evolved in modern Western history as the national state was from the welter of petty kingdoms, duchies, electorates, and archbishoprics which it succeeded. In speaking of succession I do not mean to imply that party dictatorship is the wave of the future. All of us certainly hope not. But "the age of nationalism" may not be the final chapter of human history; and whatever later chapters may record, they will certainly reveal momentous changes that have been going on, half-perceived but only half-understood, in our own time. These are matters which challenge understanding; and when we epitomize them as "individualism" (or its dreadful reverse), we are guilty of nonfeasance.

This estoppel would not be so bad were it not for the fact that when thinking stops, magic almost inevitably takes over. Nowadays very few people admit to a belief in magic. But just as few are entirely free from it. Nobody ever invokes magic to explain ordinary and commonplace events. It is only the unusual which seems to transcend the common run of cause and effect and therefore to require correspondingly transcendental explanation. The difference between ourselves and primitive peoples is largely that of the frequency with which extraordinary things happen. As Joyce Cary has said, in Africa nobody ever dies by accident. But we know all about death and even give legal status to accidental death. Like Cato the Elder, we do not suppose that we are immortal, and so have no need of magic to explain our common mortality. But let a "genius" appear—an Einstein or a Newton, a Mozart or a Michelangelo—and straightway we go off the deep end. Dazzled by these luminaries, perfectly serious scholars tell us with all the solemnity of Revealed Truth that we owe all the vast achievements of civilization to these few gentlemen (and one or two ladies).

Thus "individual" serves as a *mana* word. Like "taboo," the word "mana" has been brought into English from the Polynesian languages to designate a form of magic, in this case the magic potency with which individuals are supposed to be endowed. Savages suppose that a warrior can assimilate the *mana* of a dead opponent whose prowess was very great by drinking his blood or eating his heart. Modern scholars have no such easy explanation of the genius of a Napoleon or a Shakespeare. In this respect savagery has an advantage over modern scholarship. Savages know the procedures by which *mana* can be transferred or induced. It can be induced by scarifying initiation ceremonies through the performance of which the initiate becomes, so to speak, a marked man. He now has the *mana* of his rank. It is known and felt by all, and he is treated accordingly; whereas among us genius cannot be recognized until works of genius have been produced, and sometimes not until they have had two or three generations to soak into the apprehension of posterity. Nevertheless, so we are told, these are the creative spirits to whom we owe our civilization.

This of course is nonsense. Indeed, it is nonsense of a magnitude that is beyond any "separate" individual's capacity for error. Such a conception of genius is an authentic derivative of primitive magic. Nobody denies that luminaries are bright. Indeed, that some people are brighter than others, and some stupider than others, is a matter of common observation. The question is, how bright is brightest? If we suppose that each of these *recognized* geniuses had the highest intelligence quotient any human being has been known to have (realizing clearly that the world may have failed to recognize others such as they, perhaps because they had been committed to the Bedlams of their day), is the magnitude of such an I.Q. comparable to the magnitudes we would have to employ in measuring their celebrity and importance of their work? We measure I.Q. (however badly) on a scale of 100. On what scale should we measure the celebrity of an Einstein, or an Elizabeth Taylor? A scholar is said to be "internationally known" if his name has appeared in a footnote of a foreign publication, even though he may be known only to a few hundred other scholars in his own country and may pass unnoticed in his own home town. The name of Shakespeare has been known to millions—perhaps billions—of people over a period of ten generations or so. Is the magnitude of his presumed I.Q., or "native genius," really comparable to the magnitude of such celebrity, plotted on a scale that runs all the way from obscurity to ageless fame?

Furthermore, quite apart from issues of magnitude, both celebrity and importance are entirely different matters from native genius. The latter, however it may be defined, is by definition unaffected by the opinions or activities of others. This is what all possible definitions must have in common. But, likewise by definition, celebrity is wholly a matter of what other people know. As such it may be decisively affected by what other people do quite independently of anything the subject does. Einstein's is a striking case of a "genius" who had fame thrust upon him. His most original work, of which all his later work was a development, was published in 1904. But for fifteen years thereafter he pursued an ordinary academic career in relative obscurity. What projected him into the spotlight of world publicity was a dramatic announcement by the British Astronomer Royal that "the stars are out of place," just as Einstein had predicted. Einstein predicted other things just as important to scientists. But none proved as sensational as the apparent displacement of "fixed" stars, and none was anything like as dramatically announced. The most efficient public relations counsel could not have created a greater sensation than that achieved by the Royal Society, of which Einstein was the passive beneficiary, or victim.

The same is true of importance. The importance of every man's work is a function of what others do, including what others have already done. Everybody—scientist, artist, and the humblest hewer of wood and drawer of water—stands on the shoulders of his predecessors. How important his work is depends in significant part upon the importance of the shoulders on which he stands. How many good men have disappeared into obscurity in consequence of hitching their wagons to falling stars? The world is full of them. It is also full of quite ordinary men whose greatness is a function of subsequent events. Columbus is a figure of considerable note in the Western Hemisphere. But what if, as Columbus himself supposed, there were no Western Hemisphere? The temptation to credit men of genius with having not only foreseen but intended subsequent developments is almost irresistible and is a major factor in our inveterate misconception of the nature and role of "the individual." Even men of genius are only men. The future is concealed from them, as it is from all of us. It is reliably reported that when asked, in

1934, if man would ever "unlock the atom's energy," Albert Einstein replied, "no, never." *Sic transit gloria.*

That mankind should impute magical powers to "genius" is after all not very strange. As a species we have lived with magic, and by conjury, for something like a million years, and are pretty well accustomed to it. Over virtually the whole of this period our habit of mind has been that commonly identified as "animism"; and animism is commonly conceived as the imputation of human characteristics to nonhuman beings and even to inanimate objects. But the putative characteristics so projected are not those described by mid-twentieth-century psychology. They too are suffused with magic, and this magic has lingered especially in the human "spirit." Sticks and stones have been exorcised and have taken their places on the periodic table of the elements. Even the animals have been anatomized and geneticized. Only the "individual" remains, the unique repository of our ancestral animism.

To many people the demythologization of the human spirit means the end of human freedom; and since they love freedom, as we all do, they vigorously reject what has come to be known as "determinism." But in doing so they go far beyond the logical requirements of the case. As Heisenberg and various other modern physicists have established, even the atoms and the subatomic particles are not "determined" in any unpleasant sense.

This extraordinary controversy over freedom and determinism originated in theology. The question was: How can an omnipotent Creator mete out punishment to human beings for the waywardness with which they were created? This is a question which can be left to the theologians, many of whom resolve it very neatly by pointing out that in this case, as in all others, it is beyond the powers of the human mind to penetrate the intentions and decisions of the Creator.

As regards human punishment, fortunately, the problem is much simpler. Human punishment is meted out by courts, parents, and other disciplinary authorities on the basis of human laws. These laws, as everyone knows, are far from perfect, but they are a necessity of society. Without them life would be solitary, nasty, brutish, and short—to which even an occasional miscarriage of justice is vastly preferable. It is true that no one has any alternative to playing according to the rules of some segment of some society. Even a hermit does so. Is this bad? But no human being can be a bird or a jellyfish. By no endeavor can a magnet ever attract a silver churn. Is this bad?

The truth is that what is unpleasant about determinism and what is foolish about freedom is largely, if not altogether, a matter of words. Obviously freedom is desirable precisely because it can so easily be lost. Any state of being which by definition cannot be lost cannot be identified even negatively with freedom. No one complains about not being free from gravitation, or from oxygen. The whole meaning of freedom, insofar as it is comprehensible by the human mind, is that of the relations of human beings to each other. The antonym of "freedom" is "slavery," not "determinism"—whatever that may mean.

A trick that children sometimes play consists of one child's telling others that they are his slaves and must do everything he wills them to do. The others, of course, repudiate this power, whereupon the first immediately tells them that he has willed them to do so. They call him names. But this too he declares he has willed; and so on. But this of course is nonsense. No human being has any such power over any other human being. It is because they seem to contradict this universal truth that phenomena such as those of hypnotism, brain washing, and the like, exercise their perennial fascination. But only to a very limited degree does any such power actually exist. *Trilby* was a work of science fiction, and should have been written by Jules Verne. Certainly no determinist has ever meant to assert that human beings are zombies.

What determinists do assert is that all natural events succeed each other in unbroken continuity—in short, that nature makes no jumps. *Natura non saltum fecit.* The theory of the "indeterminacy" of the atom does not assert that atoms are causeless and thus different from all the rest of the universe. What it asserts is that atoms are just like people, in that it is impossible to predict with certainty where any one of them will be a short time hence; and this is exactly what intelligent determinists assert about people.

In this sense all scientists are determinists, though many of them demur at the use of this word—and rightly so. For, festooned as it is with the myriad uses of the verb "to determine," it almost irresistibly implies a discretionary agency, almost a master-servant relationship. This, of course, is what devotees of freedom find offensive and untrue. What they deny is untrue, of course. To assert that all human behavior is learned, just as language is learned, is not to assert that society puts words into our mouths. The differences between the words of John Keats and Edgar Guest still remain to be accounted for. Both men were denizens of a free society, and both might be said to have been victims of commercialism, though they bore its scars on quite different parts of their spiritual anatomy. Both men were "individuals." The creative fire may have burned more brightly in one than in the other; but few literary critics today attribute Keats' "inspiration" to literal demonic possession. Demonism has gone out of fashion. We are all determinists today, and all likewise believe in freedom of the will; and what has made this resolution possible is precisely our emancipation from the animism of earlier societies. We still use such words as "will" in casual conversation and in various metaphorical senses, just as we do "individual"; but the "will" has disappeared from the more meticulous vocabulary of scientists.

Curiously enough, the process of emancipation from age-old superstition which has been going on at a steadily accelerating rate throughout modern times has also come to be generally regarded as the triumph of individualism over—something else. The identity of that something else varies from one situation to another. In religion "individual conscience" seems to triumph over theocracy; in government the "individual voter" (or property owner) seems to triumph over tyranny; and in the marketplace "individual" buyers and sellers triumph over the East India Company and the Tennessee Valley Authority. All these developments do indeed have something in common. Their historical parallelism is too striking to be mistaken for coincidence. But to identify what is common to all these developments as individualism is to miss the boat completely.

Doubtless it would be an exaggeration to attribute the whole of the religious experience of Western civilization to the invention of printing from movable types, but one can scarcely exaggerate the importance of lay access to the Bible. Throughout the past, access to sacred writings had been the exclusive prerogative of priests—a monopoly which was maintained not merely by taboo but by illiteracy. Up to the middle of the fifteenth century no community had ever existed anywhere in the world in which reading and writing materials were generally accessible or in which literacy was general. The invention of printing from movable types—itself a consequence of the introduction of the

Chinese art of making identical copies from wood blocks into a region where phonetic alphabets prevailed—broke this monopoly. It has been estimated that in the ensuing half-century twenty million books were printed. We can only guess at the number of people who learned to decipher the mysterious symbols of the printed page during the same interval, but it must have been more than all the priests and scribes in all the countries of the world throughout all previous history.

These people were for the most part devout Christians. It was therefore no mere coincidence that the first book Gutenberg printed was the Latin Bible. But learning Latin was far more bothersome than learning to read: hence the fanatical eagerness with which the Bible was translated into the common speech of a dozen different linguistic communities. From this it was only a step, and an inevitable step, to sectarian particularism and to higher criticism. In short, a process had set in which has recently begun to be called "demythologization." Obviously the parallel development of modern science, from the Copernican revolution to the Darwinian revolution, has contributed vastly to this current. Indeed, the farther we go in the study of any aspect of modern religious experience, the more inadequate it seems to characterize the transformation of a whole culture as "the freeing of the individual conscience." It is that, of course, but only because it is infinitely more than that.

The same is true of our political experience. This is sometimes called the age of the common man, and such an expression is not entirely without meaning. But the evolution of Western political institutions, too, has been exceedingly complex. Democracy is not just another procedure, alternative to legitimate descent, for designating rulers. The very substance and spirit of democracy are different from those of autocracy, whether the autocrat rules by "divine right" or by the naked force of a totalitarian power system. The consent of the governed—which is the essence of democracy—is genuine and meaningful to the extent that the "sovereign people" are fully informed. Hence in large measure we owe democracy also to the spread of literacy. Mass education, imperfect as it is, has been one of the greatest achievements of modern Western civilization. Insofar as government by consent has become a reality, we owe that achievement to the spread of basic knowledge and common wisdom.

Obviously, for knowledge to be spread it must exist. Here also the inception and growth of modern science must be taken into account. If modern Americans are less superstitious than Joyce Cary's Africans, it is not only because they have been sent to school. The schools have been able to inform them that lightning is an electrical phenomenon and that disease is spread by infection; and by teaching them to read, the schools have put them *au courant* with the greatest fund of knowledge that has ever existed.

As an interpretation of the meaning and causes of modern democracy these brief paragraphs are utterly inadequate. But they are not so inadequate as the attribution of this vast and complex process to "the rise of the individual."

Most absurd, because most incantational, is the chant of "economic individualism." One of the most widely held superstitions of our time is the belief that "the free market" is the arcanum of the "individual"—or vice versa. (I put "the free market" in quotation marks because it is a mythological entity. No such place exists.) This belief is widely held for two reasons: because it serves to mask a less attractive reality, and because the general public is under the impression that great scholars have "proved"—they don't quite know what, but something that gives significance to these weirdly counterbalanced forces, "supply" and "demand."

But have they? Eli Heckscher, the great Swedish economic historian, closed the first volume of his *Mercantilism* with the remark that not the least of the merits of the then new doctrine of *laissez faire* was that coming, as it did, when statesmen were at their wits' end to know what to do about the burgeoning economy, it told them that they need not do anything. This doctrine was devised by deists like Adam Smith who believed in the "pre-established harmony" of the "natural order." Preconditioned as they were to expect to find a harmony of forces everywhere, including even the unlikely scene on which human beings scramble for a living, they made a very remarkable discovery: that every commercial transaction involves both a seller and a buyer. Obviously sellers can sell only what exists, within the limits of "natural" scarcity; and buyers will buy only what "human nature" prompts people to want. Hence the bargain at which (in a "free market") they severally arrive is one for which Nature herself is ultimately responsible; and every haggler, in seeking only the best price for his goods, the best bargain for his money, or the most lucrative investment for his hoard, "is led by an invisible hand to promote an end which was no part of his intention."

This "simple and obvious system of natural liberty," as Adam Smith called it, has undergone a degree of elaboration at the hands of later scholars which would have staggered its originators. But despite the modern array of simultaneous equations, its meaning is still substantially the same. This is still what people mean who glorify the "individualism" of the marketplace; and this is why "the free market" is so widely regarded as the ark of the covenant of individual liberty, even by people who are seeking the passage of "fair trade" laws authorizing manufacturers to set and enforce the retail prices of their products.

In short, "individual" is a thrill word. Whatever may be said of the mystique of the "free market," or of the "Protestant Reformation," or of the "welfare state," we have come a long way from medieval feudalism; and our pride of achievement is richly justified. But does it do justice to these prodigiously complex and varied developments to say that they have all been accomplished by individuals? Of course they have! But what does that explain? All those individuals, too, have been composed of just a few chemical elements, chiefly H_2O. But is individualism the answer to the riddle of human achievement? The publisher of a well-known biographical dictionary is currently featuring a quotation from Emerson in his promotional literature: "There is properly no history: only biography." With all respect to Emerson, I cannot resist seizing upon this apothegm; for exactly the reverse is true, as the biographical dictionary itself attests. It identifies these individuals with their native soil, their parents, their wives and children, with all the schools they have attended, all the positions they have held, the professional associations and private clubs to which they belong, and even, in the end, their churches. This is as it should be, indeed as it must be; for a separate individual is an abstraction unknown to experience. There is properly no biography: only history.

Such being the case, we have no choice but to be historians. If we propose to worship Great Men, then of course we must deify them. But if we seek to understand some grey eminence who has stood at the crossroads of history, our task is a historical one—not only as regards the circumstances which have determined the location of the roads but also as regards the circumstances which have produced this person and brought him to this spot. It is not their uniqueness as individuals that makes men notable but their participation in significant developments. Re-

ducing them all to the least common denominator of "individuality" is like going through life with one adjective and one
expletive.

We live in a pluralistic society and a pluralistic world. To be
literate at all we must speak a pluralistic language. All sorts of
forces are now known to be at work in the vast universe of
modern science, and all sorts of forces are at work in modern
civilization. In all of these processes human beings are involved,
each of whom, however humble, is utterly unique and all of
whom, however distinguished, are so by virtue of their participation in great events.

Except in a very unimportant sense there is no such thing as
individuality. There is only participation. Only as participants
can we understand and follow the "individuals" we most admire,
and only as movements can we advance the causes to which, for
whatever reasons, we are prepared to dedicate our lives.

◇◇

Modern Economic Realities
and Individualism[1]

PAUL A. SAMUELSON

To AN ECONOMIST the word "individualism" is tied up with *laissez faire.* Or with liberalism in the nineteenth-century Manchester School sense, as distinct from the modern American connotation of a liberal as a kind of New Dealer who is just to the left of the moving center but not quite over the brink into radicalism. Perhaps John Stuart Mill is the archetype of an individualist. And perhaps the apotheosis of individualism is that social order which Thomas Carlyle contemptuously dismissed as "anarchy plus the constable." In this last century the world has obviously moved away from rugged individualism. Presumably, in the century before that, the Western world had been moving toward a greater degree of individualism. Yet it would be a mistake to

[1] Acknowledgment is made to Felicity Skidmore for research assistance. Part of this discussion was adapted from my contribution to a Swarthmore symposium and from research for a workshop sponsored by the Industrial Relations Division of the University of California at Berkeley. See George J. Stigler and Paul A. Samuelson, "A Dialogue on the Proper Economic Role of the State," *Selected Papers,* No. 7 (Graduate School of Business, University of Chicago, 1963); also P. A. Samuelson, "Personal Freedoms and Economic Freedoms in the Mixed Economy," *The Business Establishment,* Earl F. Cheit (ed.), (New York, John Wiley & Sons, Inc., 1964), Chap. 6, pp. 193–227.

CARL A. RUDISILL LIBRARY
LENOIR RHYNE COLLEGE
HICKORY, N. C. 28601

think that there was ever a golden age of unadulterated individualism.

Eden in Equilibrium

Physicists have a model of a dilute gas. The air in this hypo-
thetical balloon I hold in my hand is supposed to consist of a
number of hard little atoms in continuous motion. So small is
each atom as to make the distances between them very large
indeed. It is a lonely life, and the encounters between atoms are
very few and far between—which is indeed fortunate since the
encounters are envisaged by the physicist as involving collisions
with elastic rebounds. Something like this is pictured by the
extreme individualist. Daniel Boone, who moved farther west
when he could begin to hear the bark of his neighbor's dog,
would regard this model of a dilute gas as very heaven. Those
who cherish family life, or at the least have an interest in biological survival, will gladly extend the notion of an individual to
include the family group. Nor will this daunt the physicist, who
is happy to think of the air in this balloon as consisting of molecules, which in their turn consist of clusters of parent-and-
children atoms rather than detached bachelors.

I will tell you a secret. Economists are supposed to be dry-as-
dust, dismal fellows. This is quite wrong, the reverse of the truth.
Scratch a hard-boiled economist of the libertarian persuasion
and you find a Don Quixote underneath. No lovesick maiden
ever pined for the days of medieval chivalry with such sentimental impracticality as some economists long for the return to a
Victorian marketplace that is completely free. Completely free?
Well, almost so. There must, of course, be the constable to ensure
that voluntary contracts are enforced and to protect the property
rights of each molecule which is an island unto itself.

Where Carlyle envisaged an anarchy that was veritable chaos, a jungle red in tooth and claw, the antiquarian economist sees Newtonian order—an impersonal system of competitive checks and balances. Life in this other Eden is neither nasty, brutish, nor short. Law, labor, and capital end up getting combined in an optimal way, so that the best menu of apples, automobiles, Picasso paintings, comic books, gin, applesauce, xylophones, and zebras is offered to the consumer. He chooses from the lot what pleases him best. As Bentham said, all pleasures are one: push-pin is as good as poetry provided individuals deem it so. Apple-jack gives a less pure pleasure than apple juice, but not for the reason that alcohol is morally bad. Rather only for the reason that its positive pleasure tonight must be carefully adjusted for the negative pleasure of tomorrow's hangover; if the net balance yields more utils than apple juice, then bottoms up! If at some midpoint between tonight's revelry and tomorrow's hangover, you decide to walk over Niagara Falls on a tightrope, that is just your way of maximizing utility. Should the enterprise turn out in some altitudinal way to have been a mistake—well, each man who is free and twenty-one is entitled to make his own mistakes without the nosy interference of his neighbor or of artificial government.

Special allowance might have to be made for lunatics and minors. While most Benthamites would certify women as "competents"—i.e., free-wills whose tastes should be respected—few of them would go as far as Albert Schweitzer and extend the felicific calculus to animals, insects, and plants. The formula, each to count for one and only one, was not expected to include chimpanzees or amoebae. The total utility which the Universe was to minimize apparently did not include an algebraic contribution from the likes of them.

On the other hand Bentham would not have recognized an inferior caste of slaves whose pleasures were not to count. What would he think of a person who sold himself into perpetual slavery in order to give a weekend *potlatch*? I am not sure, but if it were a sober, arms-length transaction at the going competitive market price, I dare say Bentham would have wanted such contracts to be legally enforceable.

What Smith Hath Wrought

The first human was Adam. The first economist (if one can make the distinction) was Adam Smith. The year 1776 was a vintage one: it gave us the Declaration of Independence, the work of Thomas Jefferson and a committee; and it gave us *The Wealth of Nations,* the work of an individual. Smith was an urbane and skeptical Scot nurtured on the same branch water as his friend David Hume. No zealot he, Smith gave two resounding cheers for individualism; but for state interference of the prenineteenth-century type, he could muster up only a Bronx cheer.

And make no mistake about it: Smith was right. Most of the interventions into economic life by the State were then harmful both to prosperity and freedom. What Smith said needed to be said. In fact, much of what Smith said still needs to be said: good intentions by government are not enough; acts do have consequences that had better be taken into account if good is to follow. Thus, the idea of a decent real wage is an attractive one. So is the idea of a low interest rate at which the needy can borrow. Nonetheless, the attempt *by law* to set a minimum real wage at a level much above the going market rates, or to set a maximum interest rate for small loans at what seem like reasonable levels, inevitably does much harm to precisely the persons whom the legislation is intended to help. Domestic and foreign experience—today, yesterday, and tomorrow—bears out the Smithian truth. Note that this is not an argument against *mod-*

erate wage and interest fiats, which may improve the perfection of competition and make businessmen and workers more efficient.

Smith himself was what we today would call a pragmatist. He realized that monopoly elements ran through *laissez faire.* When he said that Masters never gather together even for social merriment without plotting to raise prices against the public interest, he anticipated the famous Judge Gary dinners at which the big steel companies used to be taught what every oligopolist should know. Knowing the caliber of George III's civil service, Smith believed the government would simply do more harm than good if it tried to cope with the evil of monopoly. Pragmatically, Smith might, if he were alive today, favor the Sherman Act and stronger antitrust legislation or even public utility regulation generally. He might even, in our time, be a Fabian. Certainly Jeremy Bentham, with his everlasting concern for maximizing utility, would in our nonindividualistic age be a social activist— at the very least a planner of the present French type.

The Invisible Hand

One-hundred-per-cent individualists skip these pragmatic lapses into good sense and concentrate on the purple passage in Adam Smith where he discerns an Invisible Hand that leads each selfish individual to contribute to the best public good. Smith had a point; but he could not have earned a passing mark in a Ph.D. oral examination in explaining just what that point was. Until this century, his followers—such as Bastiat—thought that the doctrine of the Invisible Hand meant one of two things: (a) that it produced maximum feasible total satisfaction, somehow defined; or (b) that it showed that anything which results from the voluntary agreements of uncoerced individuals must make them better (or best) off in some important sense.

Both of these interpretations, which are still held by many

modern libertarians, are wrong. This is not the place for a technical discussion of economic principles, so I shall be very brief and cryptic in showing this. First, suppose some ethical observer —such as Jesus, Buddha, or for that matter John Dewey or Aldous Huxley—were to examine whether the total of social utility (as that ethical observer scores the deservingness of the poor and rich, saintly and sinning individuals) was actually maximized by 1860 or 1962 *laissez faire.* He might decide that a tax placed upon yachts, the proceeds to go to cheapen the price of insulin to the needy, might increase the total of utility. Could Adam Smith prove him wrong? Could Bastiat? I think not. Of course, they might say that there is no point in trying to compare different individuals' utilities because they are incommensurable and can no more be added together than can apples and oranges. But if recourse is made to this argument, then the doctrine that the Invisible Hand maximizes total utility of the universe has already been thrown out the window. If they admit that the Invisible Hand will truly maximize total social utility *provided the state intervenes so as to make the initial distribution of dollar votes ethically proper,* then they have abandoned the libertarian's position that individuals are not to be coerced, even by taxation.

In connection with the second interpretation that anything which results from voluntary agreements is in some sense, *ipso facto,* optimal, we can reply by pointing out that when I make a purchase from a monopolistic octopus, I have performed a voluntary act, for I can always go without alka-seltzer or aluminum or nylon or whatever product you think is produced by a monopolist. Mere voluntarism, therefore, is not the root merit of the doctrine of the Invisible Hand: what is important about it is the system of checks and balances that comes under perfect competition; and its measure of validity is at the technocratic level of efficiency, not at the ethical level of freedom and individualism.[2] That this is so can be seen from the fact that such socialists as Oscar Lange and A. P. Lerner have advocated channeling the Invisible Hand to the task of organizing a socialistic society efficiently.

[2] What perfectly competitive equilibrium, the Invisible Hand, achieves is this: if production functions satisfy appropriate returns conditions, if all externalities of production and tastes are appropriately absent (which includes the absence of public goods and of neighborhood effects), then competitive equilibrium is such that not *everyone* can be made better off by any intervention. This is not a theorem about ideal *laissez faire,* for it holds just as valid after good or bad (lump-sum) interferences have determined the initial distribution of wealth and earning powers. There are literally an infinite number of equilibrium states just as "efficient" as that of laissez-faire individualism. Such an efficiency state is a necessary but not sufficient (repeat, not) condition for maximization of a social-welfare function that respects individuals' tastes. It is a tribute to competitive pricing that under the severe returns and externality conditions specified, and only then, it can maximize an ethically prescribed social-welfare function, provided the initial "distribution of resources" has been rectified so as to make of equal social deservingness each consumer dollar which votes in the market. All this is complex and was not understood until this century at the earliest. A. Bergson, P. Samuelson, and O. Lange can, I think fairly, be cited for the present formulation; but parts of it had been understood, and sometimes misunderstood, by such distinguished economists as V. Pareto, E. Barone, A. P. Lerner, N. Kaldor, J. R. Hicks, and T. Scitovsky. Mention should be made of the useful intuitions of the neoclassical economists L. Walras, K. Wicksell, A. Marshall, F. von Wieser, A. C. Pigou, A. Young, J. B. Clark, P. Wicksteed, F. Edgeworth, F. Taylor, F. Knight, H. Hotelling, J. Viner, and still others. For a partial review of doctrine, see P. Samuelson, *Foundations of Economic Analysis,* Chapter Eight (Cambridge, Massachusetts: Harvard University Press, 1947).

An economist might wonder whether the later work of K. Arrow does not cast doubt on the concept of a social-welfare function. Valuable as it is in its own right as a contribution to mathematical politics, Arrow's demonstration, that it is impossible to have a "constitutional function" that compromises differing tastes of individuals and at the same time satisfies certain

In summary, these individualistic atoms of the rare gas in my balloon are not isolated from the other atoms. Adam Smith, who is almost as well-known for his discussion of the division of labor and the resulting efficiency purchased at the price of interdependence, was well aware of that. What he would have stressed was that the contacts between the atoms were *organized* by the use of markets and prices.

The Impersonality of Market Relations

Just as there is a sociology of family life and of politics, there is a sociology of individualistic competition. It is not a rich one. Ask not your neighbor's name; inquire only for his numerical schedules of supply and demand. Under perfect competition, no buyer need face a seller. Haggling in a Levantine bazaar is a sign of less-than-perfect competition. The telephone is the perfect go-between to link buyers and sellers through the medium of an auction market, such as the New York Stock Exchange or the Chicago Board of Trade for grain transactions. Two men may talk hourly all their working lives and never meet. It is alleged that many women have developed affection for the local milkman, but few romances have blossomed over a Merrill Lynch teletype.

---

plausible requirements, does not rob the Bergson formulation of its validity. A constitutional function is not a social-welfare function, even if it is given the same name as one. I should mention that Harsanyi, in the last decade, has made the notable contribution that the Bergson Social-Welfare Function can be written as additive in individuals' utilities provided certain plausible postulates about social choice in the presence of probabilities are accepted. The view that R. Coase has shown that externalities—like smoke nuisances—are not a logical blow to the Invisible Hand and do not call for coercive interference with *laissez faire* is not mine. I do not know that it is Coase's. But if it had not been expressed by someone, I would not be mentioning it here. Unconstrained self-interest will in such cases lead to the insoluble bilateral monopoly problem with all its indeterminacies and nonoptimalities.

These economic contacts between atomistic individuals may seem a little chilly or, to use the language of wine tasting, "dry." They remind one of those nunneries which receive sustenance from the outside world only through a contrivance like a dumb-waiter which bars all human confrontation. Or they are like the anthropological custom in which certain tribes trade with their neighbors by laying out, at dead of night, gifts which the others pick up and reciprocate. Presumably custom keeps the balance of trade about even, which is more than custom has been doing for the weak American balance of international payments in recent years.

This impersonality has its good side. If money talks, you and I do not have to fabricate conversation. That is one reason my wife buys our toothpaste at the self-service supermarket rather than at the corner drugstore—which as a matter of fact is no longer there, for reasons that are obvious. The prices have been equalized by Massachusetts law, and she is liberated from talking about the New England weather, being able to save her energies for our dialogues about Plato and Freud. On the other hand that Southern editor, Harry Golden of North Carolina, claims he has never bought an entire box of cigars in his life, since that would deprive him of pleasurable daily contacts. Under perfect *laissez faire*, those who want to talk about the weather have only to put their money in the telephone slot and dulcet tones will present the latest betting odds. I understand you already can call for a spiritual message each day; and if the demand warrants it, you will be able to dial for a set of random digits whenever your statistical work has soiled the old ones and calls for a fresh set.

Believe me, I do not wish to jest. Negroes in the South learned long ago that their money was welcome in local department stores. Money can be liberating. It corrodes the cake of custom. Money does talk. Sociologists know that replacing the rule of status by the rule of contract loses something in warmth; it also gets rid of some of the bad fire of olden times.

Impersonality of market relations has another advantage, as was brought home to many "liberals" in the McCarthy era of American political life. Suppose it were efficient for the government to be the one big employer. Then if, for good or bad, a person becomes in bad odor with government, he is dropped from employment and is put on a black list. He really then has no place to go. The thought of such a dire fate must in the course of time discourage that freedom of expression of opinion which individualists most favor. Many of the people who were unjustly dropped by the federal government in that era were able to land jobs in small-scale private industry. I say small-scale industry because large corporations are likely to be chary of hiring names that appear on anybody's black list. What about people who were justly dropped as security risks or as members of political organizations now deemed to be criminally subversive? Many of them also found jobs in the anonymity of private industry. Many conservative persons, who think that such men should not remain in sensitive government work or in public employ at all, will still feel that they should not be hounded into starvation. Few want for this country the equivalent of Czarist Russia's Siberia, or Stalin Russia's Siberia either. It is hard to tell on the Chicago Board of Trade the difference between the wheat produced by Republican or Democratic farmers, by teetotalers or drunkards, Theosophists or Logical Positivists. I must confess that this is a feature of a competitive system that I find attractive.

Moreover, no law prevents people from falling in love over the brokerage telephone. And the warm personal relationships that are lacking in the economic sphere can be pursued in after hours. Medieval guild crafts are not the only human associations that are worthwhile, and the price to retain them may be too high in terms of their inefficiency.

Eden Collapsed

I have now finished describing the ideal equilibrium of the gas which has individual atoms in dilute form. We have seen how a perfect model of competitive equilibrium might behave if conditions for it were perfect. The modern world is not identical with that model. As mentioned before, there never was a time even in good Queen Victoria's long reign, when such conditions prevailed.

To elucidate, let us ask what happens when we squeeze the balloon. Or, what is the same thing, if we permit a Malthusian proliferation of molecules within the same space. The gas is no longer dilute, the atoms no longer lonely.[3] The system heats up. Now the collisions are frequent and uncomfortable. It is no longer a question of hearing our neighbor's dog; we toss with insomnia while his TV blares. In revenge, our electric shaver distorts his morning symphony. For better or worse the human race has been joined.

Whatever may have been true on Turner's frontier, the modern city is crowded. Individualism and anarchy will lead to

[3] Density of population produces what economists recognize as external economies and diseconomies. These "neighborhood effects" are often dramatized by smoke and other nuisances that involve a discrepancy between private pecuniary costs and social costs. They call for intervention: zoning, fiats, planning, regulation, taxing, and so forth.

But too much diluteness of the gas also calls for social interfering with laissez-faire individualism. Thus, the frontier has always involved sparse populations in need of "social overhead capital," which in terms of technical economics jargon has the following meaning: when scale is so small as to lead to unexhausted increasing returns, free pricing cannot be optimal and there is a prima-facie case for cooperative intervention.

friction. We now have to coordinate and cooperate. Where co-operation is not fully forthcoming, we must introduce upon ourselves coercion. Now that man must obey the stop lights he has lost his freedom. But has he really? Has he lost something that he had? Was he free to race his car at the speed he wished and in the direction he wished? Of course not. He had only the negative freedom of sitting in a traffic jam. We have, by cooperation and coercion, although the arch individualist may not like the new order, created for ourselves greater freedom.

The principle of unbridled freedom has been abandoned; it is now just a question of haggling about the terms. Few will deny that it is a bad thing for one man, or a few men, to impose his will on the vast majority of mankind, particularly when that will involves terrible cruelty and terrible inefficiency. Yet where does one draw the line? At a 51-per-cent majority vote? Or, should there be no actions taken that cannot command unanimous agreement—a position which such modern exponents of libertarian liberalism as Professor Milton Friedman are slowly evolving toward. Unanimous agreement? Well, virtually unanimous agreement, whatever that will come to mean.

The principle of unanimity is, of course, completely impractical. My old friend Milton Friedman is extremely persuasive, but not even he can keep his own students in unanimous agreement all the time. Aside from its practical inapplicability, the principle of unanimity is theoretically faulty. It leads to contradictory and intransitive decisions. By itself, it argues that just as society should not move from *laissez faire* to planning because there will always be at least one objector—Friedman if necessary—so society should never move from planning to freedom because there will always be at least one objector. Like standing friction, it sticks you where you are. It favors the status quo. And the status quo is certainly not to the liking of arch individualists. When you have painted yourself into a corner, what can you do? You can redefine the situation, and I predicted some years ago that there will come to be defined a privileged status quo, a set of natural rights involving individual freedoms, which alone will require unanimity before it can be departed from.

At this point the logical game is up. The case for "complete freedom" has been begged, not deduced. So long as full disclosure is made, it is no crime to assume your ethical case. But will your product sell? Can you persuade others to accept your axiom when it is in conflict with certain other desirable axioms?

Not By Reasoning Alone

The notion is repellent that a man should be able to tyrannize over others. Shall he be permitted to indoctrinate his children into any way of life whatsoever? Shall he be able to tyrannize over himself? Here, or elsewhere, the prudent-man doctrine of the good trustee must be invoked, and in the last analysis his peers must judge—i.e., a committee of prudent peers. And may they be peers tolerant as well as wise!

Complete freedom is not definable once two wills exist in the same interdependent universe. We can sometimes find two situations in which Choice A is more free than Choice B in apparently every respect and at least as good as B in every other relevant sense. In such singular cases I will certainly throw in my lot with the exponents of individualism. But few situations are really of this simple type; and these few are hardly worth talking about, because they will already have been disposed of so easily. In most actual situations we come to a point at which choices between goals must be made: Do you want this kind of freedom and this kind of hunger, or that kind of freedom and that kind of hunger? I use these terms in a quasi-algebraic sense, but actually what is called "freedom" is really a vector of almost infinite components rather than a one-dimensional thing that can be given a simple ordering.

Where more than one person is concerned, the problem is thornier still. My privacy is your loneliness, my freedom to have privacy is your lack of freedom to have company. Your freedom to "discriminate" is the denial of my freedom to "participate." There is no possibility of unanimity to resolve such conflicts.

The notion (so nicely expounded in a book I earnestly recommend to you, Milton Friedman, *Capitalism and Freedom* [Chicago, 1962]) that it is better for one who deplores racial discrimination to try to persuade people against it than to do nothing at all, but, failing to persuade, it is better to use no democratic coercion in these matters—such a notion as a general precept is arbitrary and gratuitous. Its absurdity is perhaps concealed when it is put abstractly in the following form: If free men follow Practice X that you and some others regard as bad, it is wrong in principle to coerce them out of that Practice X; in principle, all you ought to do is try to persuade them out of their ways by "free discussion." One counterexample suffices to invalidate a general principle. An exception does not prove the rule; it disproves it. As a counterexample I suggest we substitute for "Practice X" the "killing by gas of five million suitably specified humans." Who will agree with the precept now?

Only two types would possibly agree to it: (1) those so naive as to think that persuasion can keep Hitlers from cremating millions; or (2) those who think the status quo achievable by what can be persuaded is a pretty comfortable one after all, even if not perfect. I exclude a third type who simply accept an axiom without regard to its consequences or who do not understand what its consequences are. The notion that any form of coercion whatever is in itself so evil a thing as to outweigh all other evils is to set up freedom as a monstrous shibboleth. In the first place,

absolute or even maximum freedom cannot even be defined un-
ambiguously except in certain special models. Hence one is being
burned at the stake for a cause that is only a slogan or name.
In the second place, as I have shown, coercion can be defined
only in terms of an infinite variety of arbitrary alternative stati
quo.

The precept "Persuade if you can but in no case coerce" can be
sold only to those who do not understand what it is they are
buying. This doctrine sounds a little like the "Resist not evil"
precepts of Jesus or Gandhi. But there is absolutely no true similarity between the two doctrines, and one should not gain in
palatability by being confused with the other.

Marketplace Coercion, or the Hegelian Freedom of Necessity

Libertarians fail to realize that the price system is, and ought
to be, a method of coercion. Nature is not so bountiful as to give
each of us all the goods he desires. We have, by the nature of
things, to be coerced out of such an expectation. That is why we
have policemen and courts. That is why we charge prices which
are high enough relative to limited money, to limit consumption.
The very term "rationing by the purse" illustrates the point.
Economists defend such a form of rationing, but they have to do
so primarily in terms of its efficiency and its fairness. Where it is
not efficient—as in the case of monopoly, externality, and avoid-
able uncertainty—it comes under attack. Where it is deemed
unfair by ethical observers, its evil is weighed pragmatically
against its advantages, and modifications of its structure are
introduced.

Classical economists, like Malthus, always understood this
coercion. They recognized that fate dealt a hand of cards to the
worker's child that was a cruel one, and a favorable one to the
well-born. John Stuart Mill in a later decade realized that man-

kind, not Fate with a capital *F,* was involved. Private property is a concept created by and enforced by public law. Its attributes change in time and are man-made, not Mother Nature-made.

Nor is the coercion a minor one. Future generations are condemned to starvation if certain supply-and-demand patterns rule in today's market. Under the freedom that is called *laissez faire,* some worthy men are exalted; and so are some unworthy ones.[4] Some unworthy men are cast down; and so are some worthy ones. The Good Man gives the system its due, but reckons in his balance its liabilities that are overdue.

Anatole France said epigrammatically all that needs to be said about the coercion implicit in the libertarian economics of *laissez faire.* "How majestic is the equality of the Law, which permits both rich and poor alike to sleep under the bridges at night." I believe no satisfactory answer has yet been given to this. It is certainly not enough to say, "We made our own beds and let us each lie in them."[5] For once democracy rears its pretty head, the voter will think: "There, but for the Grace of God and the Dow Jones averages, go I."

How Unequal Is Equal? Is Unequal?

The game is up for abnegation of all social decision making. To "do nothing" is not really to do nothing but to continue to do what has been done. Since coercion is willy-nilly involved, and

---

[4] "I am kept from attending college because my family is——." To discern the coercion implicit in a competitive pricing system, note that any of the following can be substituted into the blank space: Negro, bourgeois, Jewish—or, poor.

[5] If one disagrees with Malthus and France and thinks that we all had equal opportunities and *have* made the beds we are to lie in, our judgment of *laissez faire* improves—as it should. But note it is because of its fine welfare results, and *not because the kind of freedom embodied in it is the end-all of ethics.*

there is no algebraic magnitude of it that can be minimized in the interests of maximizing algebraic freedom of n men, what can abstract reasoning deduce concerning the "equitable" exercise of coercion, or, what may be the same thing, concerning the setting up of optimal arrangements for cooperation? Very little, as experience has shown and as reason itself confirms.

"Equals are to be treated equally." Who could disagree with this sage precept? But what does it mean? And how far does it carry us? No two anythings are *exactly* equal. In what respect are they to be treated as essentially equal? What differences are to be ignored? Here are two organisms, each with a nose. Should they be treated equally, and what does it mean to do so? If the state taxes a brunette a dollar, then few will argue it should tax a redhead two. That seems discriminatory. But what if the redhead has a million dollars of income or wealth and the brunette has a thousand? Many would consider it indiscriminate to treat them as equals, to tax them each the same number of dollars or the same percentage of dollars.

A true story points up the problem of defining equality as a guide to "equity." In the Second World War, Professor Ragnar Frisch, a world-famous economist and a brave Norwegian patriot, was put into a concentration camp by the Nazis. Food was scarce there and rationed. Frisch, according to legend, raised the question: Is equal rations per man equitable? Or, since nutritional need depends on metabolism which depends on body area and size, should not bigger men get larger allotments—their fair share, but no more? (If the result seems circular, a case of giving to him who hath, Frisch would no doubt be able to devise a measure of "inherent bigness." In any case no important vicious circle would be involved since the infinite series would be a rapidly converging one, as in the case where Gracie Allen found that the heavier a package was, the more stamps she had to put on it, and the heavier still it became.) This is not a trifling matter. Colin Clark has pointed out that 1,800 daily calories for a small-boned man in the tropics is not quite so bad as it sounds.

"Do unto others as you would have them do unto you." Shaw has not so much improved on this Golden Rule as given its anti-dote. "Do not do unto your neighbor as you would have him do unto you; his tastes may be different." This is, of course, the Anatole France point about asymmetry made general. It illustrates how little guidance can be derived from Kant's Categorical Imperative: Act (or create institutions that will lead to acting) in such a way that if your action were generalized to all, the total welfare and welfare of each would be maximized. Such a precept has meaning only in a perfect symmetry situation; in real life even approximate axes of symmetry cannot be found and agreed upon.

The whole matter of proper tax policy involves issues of ethics, coercion, administration, incidence, and incentives that cannot begin to be resolved by semantic analysis of such terms as "freedom," "coercion," or "individualism."

Mine, Thine, and Our'n

Life consists of minimizing multiple evils, of maximizing multiple goals by compromise. Inevitably involved is a "rule of reason." But this kind of rule is misnamed, for it cannot be generated by abstract reason. It depends on ethics and experience. I shall not labor the point but merely give some examples of the inability of deductive reasoning to infer what is the optimal pattern of freedom and coercion, of individualism and cooperation.

Mill, and anyone, will agree: You are to be as free as possible so long as you do not interfere with the freedom of others. Or as Mrs. Pat Campbell, Bernard Shaw's pen pal, put it: Anyone can do whatever he likes so long as he does not scare the horses in the street. In an interdependent world the horses scare easily.

In practice, as recent reports in Britain illustrate, the gist of these modes of reasoning leads to the view that the law should not interfere with, say, the relationships between homosexuals so long as these are carried on in private. But, as these reports say, certain special issues are connected with the problem of enticement of the young or simply enticement in general. Quite similar problems exist in connection with heterosexuality but almost escape notice in our post-Victorian world.

Let me leave this whole issue by reminding you of a well-told anecdote. A gay young blade is blithely swinging his umbrella and is told off by an irate oldster.

GAY YOUNG BLADE: What's the matter, this is a free country, isn't it?

IRATE OLDSTER: Yes, young man, but your freedom ends where my nose begins.

Actually, this is an understatement. Just as we have the rule of a three-mile limit, so there is intrinsically involved here a six-inch rule of nasal *Lebensraum*. And life is much more complicated even than this, for, just as we live by taking in each other's washing, we live by breathing in each other's breath. Abstract reasoning cannot *find* a line between individuals, nor *draw* a line.

Finale

We live in an interdependent world. Just as God knows about every sparrow that falls, Einstein's theory of general relativity shows that everything does depend on everything else: when that sparrow falls, it creates a wrinkle in space-time which changes space everywhere. The doughnut which is an individual man is a collection of cells, each of which is a collection of smaller individuals. The skin that surrounds us is thin skin.

My body is remaking itself every moment: the "I" who is talking is the heir to the "I's" that were and the sire to those that will be. Radioactive isotopes show that even our teeth are tenants on a short lease; they are remaking themselves every day, and the half life of the charter-member calcium is measured in weeks, not years. Only our serial number has soullike persistence.

Before Rousseau, people made the mistake of treating children as merely adults shrunk small. The Bible and Freud go farther and tell us that an adult is merely a child grown large. Man is imperfect, and so is woman. And so is We, Incorporated, who paternalistically put restraints upon ourselves. Not even an individual's perfections are his alone; like his imperfections, they are group-made. We entered a world we never made, and leave one we did not unmake.

Carry the notion of the individual to its limit and you get a monstrosity, just as you do if you carry the notion of a group to its limit. You get not Nietzsche's superman, nor even Mill's imperfect-perfect Victorian entitled to his own mistakes. You get Wolf Boy.

The Edward Everett Hale story of *The Man Without A Country* made a lasting impression on the boy that was I. You recall that Lieutenant Philip Nolan said in a fit of temper that he wanted never to hear the name of his country again. Fate gave him his wish; and how cruel his fate was. It would be a cruel fate likewise, I have thought, should an extreme individualist be given the wish of every child: to be able to travel anywhere with the gift of being invisible, inaudible, untouchable, and for that matter, inedible. To be condemned to dwell with mankind and never experience the interaction of others—I almost said other individuals—would be misery enow. It is not human to be such a human, and he would soon beg to join some committee, any committee.

Perhaps what I have been saying comes to this. Wherever the true home of man is, it certainly is not in Coventry.

◇◇◇

The New Individualism and the Progressive Tradition

LOUIS HARTZ

The Critical Spirit: Mencken and Roosevelt

THE TWENTIETH CENTURY has witnessed the emergence of a new kind of American individualism, the individualism of non-conformity, which actually challenges the compulsive democracy of the Lockean individualism by which the nation has centrally and historically lived.[1] The new individualism has arisen curiously, without our quite observing it. In part this is because we have needed the decade of the fifties, of the very recent past, to make it into a genuine tradition of modern American thought. Surely the work of writers like Fromm, Riesman, and Whyte, the whole assault on conformity which followed the decline of McCarthy, is basic to any evaluation of this trend. But in part its neglect is due to the fact that the link between the decade of the fifties and that of the twenties, when a similar larger individualism was advanced, has been lost from sight. For all of the variations that exist, the two eras cherished in the end a common

[1] I have developed the theoretical and historical context in which this essay is projected in *The Liberal Tradition in America* (New York: Harcourt, Brace and Company, Inc., 1955).

yearning, a common iconoclasm. The critical ardour of Mencken, the satire of Lewis, the aesthetic revolt of Brooks, were preludes to the spirit of the recent time. Both movements protested against the conformity of a bourgeois world in the name of a higher personal independence. Both developed, in a land where individualism is the national faith, a sense of individuality which went beyond that faith itself.

The sources of the new mood are complex. There has always been in America, of course, a tenuous strand of sheer moral personalism, a kind of Thoreauvian element, which has skirted the peripheries of the intellectual scene. And there can be no doubt that the national individualism of the average man, against which this element has in fact revolted, has ultimately nourished the marginal mood. But the attack on conformity in our time has vastly expanded the Thoreauvian theme and is related to decisive changes in the national experience that the twentieth century has produced. In part these changes have been internal, involving the actual loss of independence on the part of the average American through economic and organizational development. The outcry against the "organization man" is a manifestation of this development. But such domestic issues have been entangled with even larger shifts in the American experience on the world plane. The involvement of the country with a whole variety of alien cultural experiences, above all its encounter with Communism, has led to such passionate and hysterical resistance on the part of the national individualist code that the inner constraints of the code itself have become apparent. The search for a new individualism which can transcend those restraints,[2]

[2] The attack on organization has an ambivalent relationship to the larger issue of the moral constraints of the national tradition. In one sense it seeks to rescue the historic individualism of the tradition, but in another it revolts against a kind of conformity to which that tradition is by no means antago-

which can insure intellectual liberty and welcome the diversity of
world experience, has arisen inevitably. It was not accidental that
the specific question of conformity defined itself immediately
after the collapse of McCarthyism during the fifties or that the
same spirit emerged during the twenties out of the constricted
intellectual atmosphere that accompanied the First World War
and the initial impact of the Bolshevik Revolution.

The new individualism has had a peculiar relationship to the
Progressive tradition. In one sense there has been a kind of
sympathy between the two movements, for they have alike
satirized the excesses of American capitalist Whiggery in the
twentieth century. Babbitt has been an enemy of them both; so
has the tradition of Harding and Coolidge. Moreover it is the
fate of Progressivism in a liberal society that even though it
subscribes to the liberal premise, its reformist use of the state lays
it open to the hyperbolical charge of collectivism. The New
Dealer has suffered more from Red-scare conformism than has
his opponent, so that he has tended instinctively to appreciate the
individualist demand for sheer intellectual liberty. And yet, despite this, there is a sense in which Progressive tradition has been
the greatest threat to the new individualism. For the iconoclasm
of the Progressive, which seeks to repair the Horatio Alger
mechanism of American life, seeks indeed to hide doctrinal
challenges to it, threatens always to take away the moral thunder
of nonconformity and to subordinate it to the very uses of the
national liberal tradition. It was not Coolidge who put Mencken
out of business, nor was it even Attorney General A. Mitchell

---

nistic. The historic sense of collective orthodoxy in the American bourgeois
faith, agitated in our own time by ideological challenge, flows into the
organizational spirit. This confluence is why the personalism of the organizational criticism has been able to blend so easily with the personalism that
has arisen out of the larger concern with civil and intellectual liberty.

Palmer, who raided the mails in the name of Americanism after the First World War. It was Roosevelt, the master pragmatic repairman of the Alger faith. The New Deal recruited to the Progressive phase of that faith the Nietzschean enthusiasm of the twenties which had begun to peer beyond it. Mencken was defeated by a kind of boring from within his own critical ranks.

It would be absurd, historically, to complain about this shift. The personalist revolt of the twenties, even its splendid expatriate cosmopolitanism, was based on the presence of an economic margin. Coolidge was assailed by the Young Intellectuals but the prosperity over which he presided was a prerequisite of the kind of criticism he received. Once the crash came, the reformist imagination was bound to become less contemptuous of economic concerns. Given American history, moreover, it was bound to search for a solution to the economic problem in terms of the historic liberal reform of the West, which is what modern American Progressivism really is, a Lloyd George effort to retain the bourgeois promise even at the moment that the state is being used. There was an instant when socialism, something perhaps like the Labor Party, seemed possible, and the hopes of Norman Thomas soared, but the visceral drift of the national tradition was all against it. The Nietzschean individualism of Mencken and Lewis was bound to go, but it was bound to be replaced not by Marx but by the narrower individualism of the American past against which it had revolted.

But if one can hardly lament this contraction of perspective in the thirties, one has a right to ask whether the determinisms behind it are a permanent aspect of the relationship between the new individualism and the Progressive tradition in the twentieth century. Indeed, given the unfolding of that relationship since the New Deal era, one can even ask whether Progressivism can survive at all unless it borrows rather than submerges the larger

vision of the other tradition. For two things have happened.
The sheer fact of economic catastrophe which killed the spirit of
the twenties has declined as an issue in our lives, while the forces
behind the new individualism have expanded enormously in
significance. Even while poverty looms as a problem, we cannot
fail to see that the concern with sheer subsistence which sus-
tained Roosevelt, and which animated the Progressive tradition
in his time, is no longer enough to support the New Deal faith.
At the same time, the issues of organization and of intellectual
liberty, those pressures to transcend the old individualism that
have arisen out of new experience, both domestic and foreign,
have become permanent. Can the Roosevelt tradition, under
these circumstances, retain its reformist personality unless it
responds to those pressures rather than undermines them as it did
before? Can it serve as an instrument of realistic innovation
unless it goes beyond its former commitments?

I believe that there is a chance of synthesis here, of a blending,
as it were, of the twenties and the thirties, which can not only
revitalize Progressivism but open up a possibility for true political
philosophy.

The Roots of the National Creed

IN AMERICAN HISTORY the conformist quality of the national
faith is an unfolding thing and we do not have it in contemporary form until after a good deal of time has passed, until after
Jackson, after the Civil War, although both of these symbolize
decisive steps in its development. This is not to say that its root,
as William Graham Sumner once saw, was not actually in the re-
strictive sides of colonial puritanism. But for a long period it is
challenged by at least marginal symbolisms: the aristocratic ethos
of the Whiggery of Hamilton and the early Adamses, the Spartan economic ethic of Jefferson and Taylor. It is only when these

dissolve, when Whiggery takes on a democratic aspect and Jeffersonian democracy an overtly capitalist aspect, that the mythology of the nation congeals into the perfect "Americanism" of Horatio Alger and Andrew Carnegie. Actually the term "Americanism" does not itself come into real play until the twentieth century with the emergence of radicalism and the impact of world events. There is an implicit nationalism here all along, but it is a part of the relaxation of the earlier time that it rarely becomes evident.

In this context the evaluation of the "conservatism" of Hamilton and the "radicalism" of Jefferson acquires a new complexity. In one sense these moods, whether they involve the yearning for a House of Lords or the dream of a quiet, nonspeculative agrarianism, are sheer fantasies of the national history. There were no lords in America, and the people from the outset were entrepreneurs, both facts being very closely related to one another. As the democratic capitalism of the Alger theme thrust itself forward through the Jacksonian era and the Civil War into the time of the late nineteenth century, it was as if the reality of the national character was finally manifesting itself. But in another sense the very cherishing of the Whig and Jeffersonian dreams gave a touch of complexity, of diversity, to the American ethical spectrum which it lost when every man high or low had to engage in Darwinian battle at the pain of being "un-American." In the earlier period, if a man wanted to escape the anxieties of that struggle, after either the fashion of Hamilton or John Taylor, at least these figures were there to back him up. To be sure, very few did, which is why both aristocracy and economic puritanism went rapidly by the board.

Of course one cannot say of these pre-Alger ethics of left and right that they fundamentally deviated from Lockean tradition itself. They did not represent true alternatives to a Lockean way of life, as let us say the ethics of Bonald and Marx did in Europe. They were forms of the liberal experience but, being both the conservative and the radical extremities of it, they showed some challenge to its central core. The early Hamiltonian Whig, or for that matter the less industrial and more agrarian Whig of the Adams school, did not so much seek the lordly life for himself as he yearned to have it about him, a kind of support on which he might rest in case the populace revolted. For his own part he was committed to liberal values if not to their democratic consequences. As for the John Taylor radical, his image of life did not even involve the presence of nonliberal social components. If we discount for the moment the "aristocratic" side of Taylor, and concentrate on his notion of the Spartan yeoman, all that is involved here is a less dynamic capitalism, a less intense economic vision. It is still individualistic and still capitalistic in the sense that the yeoman owns his own farm, casts his own vote, has the care of his own fate. Of course this is obscured by the riotous polemic of the age, in which the Taylor tradition assails "capitalists," but that polemic must be accounted the most tenuous of moral alternatives to Locke, being almost wholly a strategic blow in the battle against Whiggery.

Indeed this failure of American left and right in the early era to disentangle themselves from the central drift of liberalism made inevitable the end of their marginal deviations and the triumph of the capitalist heart of Locke. Those deviations could not get a grip on the culture, could not sink a root from which to grow. It was not merely that the early Whig literally could not find a House of Lords for whatever purpose he had in mind; it was also that his avowed concern with the possibility of one discredited him radically in an individualist world, opened him to the charge of "aristocracy" himself. I have mentioned the way in which in our time, the Progressive tradition is curiously disadvantaged by Americanism because in seeking to utilize the state, if only to repair the Alger mechanism, it is open to the charge of socialism or communism. There is some ironic compensation here, because in the time of Jefferson the Progressive tradition did precisely this to Whiggery: it tagged it with the false label of aristocracy and read it out of the American world. Even before Americanism was consciously articulated, Jefferson used it. And, of course, the early Whigs had less ground for resisting this technique than the erstwhile New Dealer does today, since their "un-Americanism," unlike his own, served very few empirical uses. Roosevelt may have saved the country by using the state, but did Hamilton accomplish anything by dreaming of a titled elite? Indeed not only was that dream useless, but the liberalism of the culture meant that the other roles Whiggery had in Europe, forging an antifeudal Enlightenment or defying a threatening mob, were also missing here.

And yet the tables are in the end turned: Whiggery, nonconformist to begin with, becomes finally the champion of the national ethic. This happens precisely because the Taylor marginalia go by the board, because the American democrat gives way to the acquisitive impulse on a larger scale. For once he has given way, Whiggery can capture him by doing only one thing: promising him that he can join its ranks through effort, that he can become the classical millionaire. This change means, to be sure, a grand democratization, a Harrison campaign replete with cider, or more tragically, a Civil War in the course of which Lincoln converts Whiggery into idealist Republicanism. But once this is done, Whiggery gains control of the national liberal club because in fact it is more authentically democratic than Democracy. Then it not only feeds the American democrat's love of equality, as Taylor did, but his love of gain, as Taylor did not. It capitalizes on the unreality of Jefferson's economic puritanism, just as Jefferson capitalized on the fantastic nature of the earlier Whig aristocratic dream. The American law of Whig compensation has an infinite variety of facets. One is to achieve for Whiggery through popular greed a grip on the nation which it could not achieve in America through revolutionary action against an *ancien régime.* From its point of view the capitalist appetite is a curious substitute for the appeal of the liberal revolution.

But the main thing accomplished is that Whiggery now becomes the possessor of the keys to the national absolute. In retrospect it is as if, in and through the victory of Jacksonian Democracy and of Republicanism, a kind of platonic telos was fulfilling itself in American history in the course of which the ambiguities at the margins of the Lockean ethic were being sloughed off and its simple core becoming victorious. Alger is Locke purified and American history, as it were, "realized." In some sense this development is a kind of progressive Declaration of Independence from Europe, an extended 1776, for the marginal ambiguities are tendrils of a larger world clinging still to the liberal element which was extracted from Europe and brought to America in the seventeenth century. The aristocratic involvements of the Whigs, the yeoman ethos of the Democrats, look back to an earlier European setting, in which the Lockean ethic was entangled. Perhaps this background explains why the elimination of both of these, the triumph of the inner substance of Locke in the Alger legend, is a drift toward the emergence of conscious Americanism. In any case, here we have the national faith, paradoxically compulsory in face of its individualism, with which America entered the twentieth century.

The Twenties and After

For that faith the decade of the nineteen twenties was a decade both of brilliance and disaster. The Alger system, buttressed by prosperity, reached an almost dizzy peak of success and the articulation of its premises became a mere matter of reciting the obvious. At the same time the First World War and the Russian Revolution had thrust that system into a terrifying alien world, which is why, together with the complacency of the Republican presidents, there was a note of hysteria, registered in the Red scare and the Palmer raids. And this in turn was matched by the sudden outburst of Mencken and the new individualists, who contributed a note of cosmic anger to the entire picture. Alger's triumph in the twenties was feverish, and there were clear premonitions of disaster.

There is irony in the fact that after the European fringes of the American tradition had been successfully eliminated, the international impact should involve it with Europe and indeed the world on a more challenging scale than before. For, of course the Kaiser was more threatening to the inner core of Locke than the aristocratic yearnings of Fisher Ames had been, and Lenin was more dire a catastrophe for the capitalist spirit than was the nonspeculative yeoman ethos of the doctrinaire Jefferson. Moreover, needless to say, neither of these new Europeanisms could be eliminated in quite the way the others were, by an unfolding of the internal logic of the American community in the form of a democratic upsurge or a Whig transformation. The American community might do anything it pleased, but the Russian Revolution would remain. Indeed the hysterical phases of American response to that Revolution revealed the difference. Jefferson and Jackson both successfully utilized nationalistic liberalism against the elitist aspirations of the early Whiggery. But the outcry of the Red-scare Americanists, with the image not of Hamilton but of a Russian Bolshevik before them, was both more intense and less successful.

Of course the exaggeration of this nationalism, which betrayed anxiety, was accompanied by an exaggeration of the dynamic premises of the Alger system in a mood of sheer confidence. There is very little to match the spirit of certainty concerning the domestic efficacy of the American scheme immediately before the crash. Hoover spoke in terms of the progress theory of history, arguing that America had come closer to the projected fulfillment of human development than had any other country at any other time. Of course there was, as Walter Lippmann noted, a peculiarly puritanic role which the Republican presidents played in the national symbolism in the midst of the boom, revealed better perhaps by Coolidge than by Hoover. This role was to enunciate the conscience of the country at the moment it was indulging in what was in fact a speculative orgy. Alger may have reached fruition in the twenties, but his success was not quite within the context of the virtues stressed in the life of Ragged Dick. Granted that some luck had always been a component of the classical Alger success story, hard work was being replaced by sheer good fortune. Or to put the matter differently, the Jeffersonian notion of economic simplicity which Alger himself had buried was buried deeper than ever.

In such a setting a sheer dialectic of extremes was involved in the emergence of Mencken: when the grip of the Tocquevillean majority had become so strong, would not a natural impulse assert itself for extrication from that grip, especially since both Palmer and Coolidge were insisting on "individualism"? Mencken's Nietzscheanism may itself have reflected the American individualism of the twenties, for the dream of sheer wealth and economic bigness had a transcendent quality about it. Spencer, at least after the Civil War, had always by virtue of the gargantuanism of the evolutionary conception been peculiarly appropriate as a rationalizer of American economic struggles. But of course Nietzsche was for Mencken a denier and not an affirmer of the national democratic ethic: it was not a transcendent millionaire but a man who transcended the millionaire himself whom the critical individualists of the twenties worshipped. Or to put the matter perhaps more precisely, they worshipped the man who transcended the dream of becoming a millionaire—the classic dream of the Alger democracy. They disliked, not the bourgeoisie, but to use Mencken's unforgettable term, the "booboisie."

This individualism seemed antipolitical, not merely because it repudiated politicians in general, as Mencken did, but precisely because it focused on the inarticulate social compulsions involved in the bourgeois world—compulsions which politics could not apparently touch. Granted that Prohibition might be repealed, could one do anything politically about the larger spirit of puritanism with which all evil was identified and against which the twenties rebelled? Mencken spoke longingly about the aristocrats of Europe, not because they provided a type of political paternalism, but because they represented a bulwark against the cultural and social commands of the democracy. Lewis did not have this concern with European elitism, although he was aware that Main Street did not thrive so easily abroad because class reality there was more complex. But was not his message, again, essentially personal?

Perhaps this personalism was why the new individualism had no real theory of American society or history. It may have spoken of puritanism, but whatever the concept meant, it was only loosely projected backward into the American past. Bernard De Voto later assailed the vagueness of the concept and he was surely justified in doing so. Of course, if puritanism had been taken in the largest sense, as the theological root of a bourgeois community, it might have provided a point of departure for the exploration of the entire emergence of the American absolute:

its origin, its fulfillment in the triumph of Jackson, and the post-Civil War resolution of American history. But this wider analytic concern is missing: puritanism is a matter of ethical constraint of "morality." Actually the individualism itself of the new individualists was vague enough in content. What was the final upshot of the revolt against the "booboisie," against Babbitry in social terms? What code of life did the new independence really involve? Mencken spoke of "civilized enlightenment," a generous but undefined phrase.

Perhaps these theoretical defects together with the collapse of prosperity and the re-emergence of Progressivism, were involved in the final deflation of the movement. Of course Roosevelt did not fully replace Mencken. The criticism of Main Street and its shibboleths was carried on by the New Deal: I have already referred to the element of community here. But the way in which Roosevelt corroded the new individualism becomes obvious once his larger relationship to it is explored. He himself had not in the twenties been an apostle of the Menckenite revolt: he had lived with the Democratic Party successfully enough, sharing its submission to the dominant Republican themes. But that is not the point. The point is that when he led the Party to the left, he made the iconoclastic energy of the twenties "responsible," which meant its immersion again from the Progressive angle in the subjectivity of the American faith. One can contend that the New Deal was in fact an empirical revolt against that faith in the name of a new collectivism. But its very empiricism was the clue to the whole matter, for it betrayed the fact that Roosevelt did not dare doctrinally to recognize the degree of collectivism he was in fact manufacturing. Hoover wanted him to do so, to concede that he was departing from "American Individualism," although Hoover was not, to be sure, concerned with philosophy but with shrewd Republican strategy. The fact that Roosevelt was able to avert that plea, to repair the Lockean machinery without repudiating Locke, was a central part of his success. He made the New Deal possible by an implicit submission to the national consensus. When he superseded Mencken and Lewis he buried them beneath the norms they had tried to criticize.

The nonconformist spirit of the fifties, which followed the Second World War and McCarthyism, was in many respects so different from the spirit of the twenties that there are sure to be some who will deny the continuity between the two moods. The undisciplined outbursts of the Prohibition decade have been replaced by Professor Riesman's deeper and more penetrating quest for "autonomy." Mr. Whyte's outcry against the organization man has a touch of the Menckenite violence, but it is grounded in a much more elaborate sense of the collective limits that modern life imposes upon private action. And yet are not these very changes proof of a greater maturity, an access of sophistication in the twentieth-century American tradition of personalism? Could we speak of such a tradition meaningfully if these changes had not been made? Certainly we cannot deny that the spirit of nonconformity in the fifties sought, as it did earlier, to transcend the narrower individualism out of which the norms of the nation had been created. The individualism which flourished after McCarthy, complex as it may have been, was neither the individualism of Hoover nor of Roosevelt, of one side or another of the Alger faith that had emerged in American history and had flowed into the McCarthy tradition itself. It was an individualism which, as in the twenties, looked toward a larger personalism and, not accidentally, it focused upon a whole series of social constraints outside politics which reflected the dominion in the country of the bourgeois norm. If Tocqueville emerged as the major hero of this concern, replacing Mencken's Nietzsche, this does not alter the point. Indeed his new significance showed an access of depth, or at least of specificity, in what is becoming a familiar American ideal of our century. Tocqueville, in his description of America, seized on precisely the force of that moral unanimity against which the larger individualism is revolting.

One is tempted, indeed, to speculate whether the popularity of writers like Tocqueville and Mill in the recent past does not symbolize, in a curious way, a kind of birth of political philosophy in the American climate. It is a commonplace that the classic philosophies of European politics have been records of aspiration: Rousseau's general will flourishing in the disintegrated structure of French politics, Benthamite individualism in the corporate world of Britain. The experience of aspiration in this sense has been missing in America, something which is typified in the very universality of liberal convictions. Aspiration has been rather a product of foreign observers, men who have been less satisfied with liberal compulsions than has the American himself, so that in a curious sense we can say that our political philosophy has had to be produced on the outside. Tocqueville was perhaps the greatest of these "American" political philosophers and outsiders. But when he moves to the center of the American intellectual stage itself, does he not become, as it were, an authentic Rousseau, an authentic Bentham—the American himself expressing, dialectically, a yearning to transcend the limits of his experience. One might perhaps say that this is the beginning of "utopianism" in American thought, the projection of a limit of the culture into a formulation of culture itself. Historically, America has worked with the materials of an individualism which in Europe was largely utopian, but, transforming that individualism into operational reality, for itself it lacked utopia. Locke was "real" here. The new individualism is more philosophic because less real than the old.

Progressivism and the Critical Temper

But will it die again at the hands of the Progressive tradition? Or will that tradition, having lost its basis in sheer economic catastrophe and having inherited the domestic and world problems that the new individualism reflects, gain itself a new mood from the absorption of that individualism? One is inspired to suggest that the brief years of the Kennedy Administration, bridging the transition from the fifties to the sixties, reflected such a mood— the animation of the Roosevelt tradition both at home and abroad by a sense of the possibility of an experience much wider than that permitted by the historic mandates of the American liberal faith. But if this is so, those years were the beginning of a long epoch of invention and redefinition for Progressivism. The appropriation of the critical spirit that has emerged in the twentieth century will carry the Progressive tradition far from its old moorings, quite a distance indeed "outside America."

The notion that the new individualism is intrinsically apolitical ought not to be misinterpreted. There cannot, of course, be a legislative program to insure personal independence as there is a Social Security program to insure unemployment compensation. But even in the case of the old Progressivism, the final goal was not "legislated": state action was undertaken in order to make Alger real—public policy which presupposed the autonomous action afterward of the individual entrepreneur. The Progressive tradition has long been habituated to the notion that state action is designed, in the phrase of the English idealists, to hinder hindrances to the right kind of private action. The question is what is right: the Greek conformity of the Alger world, or a liberation of value perspective beyond it? Progressivism can view itself as triggering the latter just as much as triggering the former. And in connection with policies that go beyond the remedy of sheer want, that deal with education or automation or even the issue of civil rights, the shift of conception is almost a necessity, whether one is a Progressive or not. Alger makes sense in connection with employment, but what does he have to say about the use of leisure time? It is interesting to notice how the transformation of Jefferson into Alger by the synthesis of the Civil War chained Progressivism more directly to scarcity values in an economic sense. Of course the American democrat now became involved in the dream of a larger wealth, the classical million dollars, but what hope did Alger offer him after the million was made? Simply to make another. It was as if the Marxian world of economic struggle, individualized and classless, were made unending, without even that leap which Marx promises from scarcity to abundance, from necessity to "freedom." For the American Progressive to think of freedom in this sense is a new adventure.

I have spoken of the English idealists and their conception of the state as an agent for the release of personality. Actually their relevance may be even wider, for that conception bears in its relationship to the blunt economics of Benthamism somewhat the same relationship that a Progressivism charged with the new individualism bears to the classical Progressivism of the New Deal. But if this is so, the transcending of Bentham in the American context involves a peculiarity: a transcending of America, precisely because the Alger ideal is not a philosophy here but a national tradition. It involves, to use the phrase in a way different from Theodore Roosevelt's, a new nationalism. And it is of course on the world plane that this new nationalism is most apparent. But is not the need to confront cultural variety even more acute here than on the domestic plane? Alger has little to say about leisure, but does he have as much to say about China? His only message, the message of the classical Locke, is isolationism, messianism, or hysteria—anything to avoid the sight of alien experience. But that sight is basic to our lives now, permanent in its necessity. It is this, more than anything else, which thrusts Progressivism out of the traditional framework, forces the impact upon it of the new critical perspectives of the century.

This synthesis resolves a problem which the Progressive has felt ever since the great iconoclastic and cosmopolitan outburst of the twenties. He himself, in one part of his mind, has cherished that mood and even though the obscurantism, or pragmatism, of the New Deal compelled him to give it up, he was not always easy in his own heart about it. Mencken and Lewis represented a part of his conscience. Life within the liberal absolute, which involves not mentioning collectivist departures from it, piously cherishing the Alger man, has often been hard. But as this form of "responsibility" loses much of its responsible tone, even its relevance, does not a chance exist for a unification of the Progressive psyche, a synthesis of the perspectives both of cultural criticism and Progressive reform?[3] Actually this unification is merely a form of responsibility to other facts in the national experience, and the new individualism, or the new nationalism, has never been the detached luxury which its critics have often made it out to be. In the end the Progressive has responded to it for the

---

[3] The problem of the unity of the Progressive outlook is peculiarly relevant in the realm of historiography. The "conflict" theory of the Progressives has been repudiated by many who continue to cherish classic Progressive norms. But this repudiation, which has actually often been exaggerated, reflects a groping for a conception of the total national experience which in the end calls for a new view of Progressivism itself. One gives up more than an historical bias when one surrenders J. Allen Smith. Conversely, those who cling to the old Progressive historiography but seek to redefine Progressive norms in terms of a transcending of the national experience are hamstrung in the effort. For the Smith pattern gives them nothing but a series of Jacksonian upsurges which it is their duty to repeat, all "within" the national history.

same reason that he has responded to the New Deal, because it solves a problem in his experience, arising from the fact that he approaches experience with a humane temper, a critical outlook.

And yet if Progressivism breaks with the historic Locke, in the end there is an ironic sense in which it does so, because of Locke himself. I have noted the way in which the new individualism is nourished by the old, and surely it is interesting to observe that individualism has appeared in no other country in the same force. Tocqueville has moved to the center of American thought, but not in the same way to the center of French thought. Mill has become an American preoccupation, but not in the same way an English one. If this development is the mark for us of "political philosophy," it is ours peculiarly, precisely because the issue of a richer individualism is for us a matter of national perspective, a problem defined by the national inheritance.[4] What is the Promise of American Life? Croly's phrase has fascinated the Progres-

---

[4] American thought on this score betrays, with an odd clarity, the whole comparative relationship of a liberal society to modern Europe. The realization of classical liberalism in America meant that the mass constraints stressed by the neoliberals of Europe would not be assailed because they were so perfectly actualized that they were not even felt to be constraints. But once they were discovered, under twentieth century circumstances, the arguments of the neoliberals were bound to assume greater importance than in Europe, not only because the problem was more vivid but because the individualist ethic which originally fed that argument—apart from any conservative influences—was a national principle. It is as if American history manifested with greater intensity but vastly more slowly the vicissitudes of European liberalism: Bentham symbolizing the drift of our history, Mill appearing in the twentieth century. There is, however, one additional matter which touches both the issues of the foreign observer and political philosophy. Bentham was implicit, the basis of operational Americanism, whereas Mill is not only himself explicit but makes Bentham so for the first time as a result of his criticism. The development, in addition to being more intense and more delayed, is characterized by an almost Hegelian expansion of consciousness.

sive, clung to his mind, for it suggests the presence of an unfulfilled element in American history which it is his mission to fulfill. May not this element be individualism itself, cut loose from the conformist framework, seen after three centuries of familiarity in an unfamiliar light?

❖❖❖

American Individualism in the Twentieth Century

DAVID M. POTTER

AT THE BEGINNING of his essay, "Individualism Reconsidered," David Riesman remarks, "Such terms as 'society' and 'individual' tend to pose a false as well as a shifting dichotomy."[1] We might take Riesman's remark and extend it by observing that, in general, we tend to discuss questions too much in terms of antitheses, and frequently in terms of antitheses which are deceptive. Thus, we speak in polarities about liberty versus authority, dissent versus conformity, and, of course, individualism versus collectivism. But in fact we know all the while that no one intends to choose starkly between these alternatives. Liberty would be intolerable to the most independent-minded person without some measure of authority, or dissent without some conformity. In fact, human life presents us with a whole series of situations in which diverse and, to some extent, conflicting values must be kept in some kind of working relationship with one another. Two junior officers both bucking for promotion will presumably work together for

---

[1] David Riesman, *Individualism Reconsidered, and Other Essays* (Glencoe, Illinois: Free Press, 1954), p. 26.

the improvement of their unit while they work in rivalry with one another for advancement. Indeed, the principle of "antagonistic cooperation" probably goes much deeper than this, for even nature seems to abound in situations where two elements are linked in a relationship of tension and at the same time of interdependence. The basic case is the relationship of men and women, eternally needing one another and eternally engaged in a "battle of the sexes"; but there is also the case of youth and age, with youth forever restive under its dependence upon the elders, and the elders forever vexed by the brashness of a youth which they have lost, and with each unwillingly drawing upon the other for qualities which it, itself, lacks. Along with these classic dualisms, there is also the relationship between man alone, and man in society—man constantly straining against the compulsion imposed by the group, and man continuously driven by need for identity with the group. These conflicting needs must forever be mediated and accommodated, and the ultimate choice of either one to the complete exclusion of the other would be equally unthinkable. In our literature, any story of the complete isolation, either physical or psychological, of a man from his fellow man, such as the story of Robinson Crusoe before he found a human footprint on the beach, is regarded as essentially a horror story. But the tale of any man having his identity completely swallowed up by total absorption into the group, as happened for the members of the Party in Oceania in George Orwell's *1984*, is also regarded as a kind of nightmare.

If this principle of balance or beneficent tension between conflicting values has any validity in the cases which I have mentioned, it might be argued that it has even more in the case of individualism, especially in the United States. For is it not notoriously true that historically American individualism has always been sanctioned only within very sharply defined limits? The

word "individualism," of course, has been included in our litany
of sacred terms, and in many respects, America has placed an im-
mense premium upon the individualistic values of independence,
self-reliance, and rejection of authority. But American society has
never, I believe, sanctioned the attempt of a person to practice the
kind of individualism which one would find in a society with a
recognized elite. An elite or aristocratic individualist is likely to
regard the principles of individualism as conferring a franchise
for self-indulgence as well as for self-expression. This was the
kind of individualism which Lord Byron practiced—the kind
which he defended in his epic of Don Juan. It lends itself to the
idea that the talented man may become a superman and that he is
quite justified in sacrificing less talented men and in riding
roughshod over them. Nietzsche is unfavorably remembered for
exalting this superman version of individualism, and of course
one finds the ideal set forth also in Shaw's *Man and Superman*.

Individualism in this form seems profoundly alien to the
American tradition—so alien that we who are in the American
tradition do not usually even recognize it as a form of individualism. Yet occasionally we will find a traveller from overseas who
regards individualism as involving the right of the individualist
to indulge his own impulses at the expense of others, to attain
self-expression regardless of its effect on other people. Such a
person is astonished that American individualism carries no such
franchise. The writings of Tocqueville abound in observations
on the lack of real variety in American life, despite all its claims
to individualism. But the most vivid statement of the point that I
think I have ever seen was made by Tocqueville's compatriot,
Michael de Chevalier, also in the 1830s:

As for us [the French], who resemble each other in nothing except in
differing from everybody else, for us, to whom variety is as necessary as
the air, to whom a life of rules would be a subject of horror, the Yankee

system would be torture. Their liberty is not the liberty to outrage all that is sacred on earth, to set religion at defiance, to laugh morals to scorn, to undermine the foundations of social order, to mock at all traditions and received opinions. It is neither the liberty of being a monarchist in a republican country, nor that of sacrificing the honor of the poor man's wife or daughter to one's base passions; it is not even the liberty to enjoy one's wealth by a public display, for public opinion has its sumptuary laws, to which all must conform under pain of moral outlawry; nor even that of living in private differently from the rest of the world.[2]

Just how serious Chevalier was in asserting the right to seduce a poor man's wife as one of the prerequisites of individualism in its Gallic form, I do not know. But his mere voicing of this assertion gives us, I believe, a kind of benchmark which may help to define the limits of individualism in its Yankee form. This assertion of individualism would not do at all for Americans; and why, we may ask, would it not? Why are Chevalier's suggestions more or less offensive to us, and why, particularly, does the suggestion about the poor man's wife grate on us more than the proposal to "outrage all that is sacred"? I would suggest that it is because Chevalier is implicitly denying the American proposition that men are intrinsically equal, even though their physical circumstances may vary immensely. For a rich man to seduce the wife of another rich man might be accepted in a spirit of joviality, under the axiom that all is fair in love and war, but for him to seduce the wife of a poor man is to treat a fellow man as less than an equal simply because he is poor. In the American creed this is, perhaps, the sin against the Holy Ghost.

It may seem that I am dwelling too much here upon what may have been a random phrase in the writing of one Frenchman now dead for more than a century, but I have lingered over it

[2] John William Ward (ed.), *Society, Manners, and Politics in the United States: Letters on North America by Michael Chevalier* (Garden City, New York: Doubleday & Company, Inc. [Anchor Books], 1961), pp. 327–328.

because I believe it may illustrate, in a particularly vivid way, the fact that American individualism has always been limited and held in balance by other cherished principles which were not entirely consistent with it. It could never be asserted in a way which would violate the principle of equality, and we will do well to look twice before we even assume that it placed the values of man in isolation ahead of the values of man in a group, or man in society.

Thus far I have avoided attempting a definition of individualism, on the theory that by some principle similar to Parkinson's Law, the number of different definitions of any valuative term in any academic symposium will increase in direct ratio to the number of participants on the panel. But at this point it may be necessary for me to pause and declare myself as to what I understand individualism to have meant in American life. If so, I must venture an assertion that American individualism in the nineteenth century and American individualism in the twentieth century have had two fundamentally different emphases, but that both of them have placed great weight upon the belief that individualism should serve as a means to group welfare rather than as a way of exalting man in isolation. This assertion may be difficult to prove, but let us examine it. To specify more fully, let me suggest that the individualism of the nineteenth century stressed the element of self-reliance while that of the twentieth century has stressed the element of nonconformity or dissent, but that in each case there was a strong emphasis upon the value of the quality in question for society as a whole and not simply for the individual apart from society.

Theoretically, perhaps, it might be supposed that these two emphases are not very different: that self-reliance and nonconformity would go together and would tend to converge. It is logical to argue that a man who does not depend on other people for his physical welfare will certainly not be very quick to borrow his ideas from them. If he has the habit of fending for himself, will he not also have the habit of thinking for himself? If he shows initiative in his endeavors to attain success, will he not also show initiative in forming his social ideas? If individualism equals independence and independence equals freedom and freedom equals dissent, then doesn't it follow that individualism equals dissent? Perhaps the plausibility of this kind of equation has led us to the fallacy of using one term, "individualism," to express the ideas of both self-reliance and nonconformity.

But history often mocks logic, and in our historical experience, the believers in self-reliance, in the sense of taking care of oneself, and the believers in nonconformity, in the sense of encouraging dissent, have often been far, far apart. In fact, these two types of individualists seem to be almost natural antagonists, for the "rugged individualist" of laissez-faire economics is likely to be what we call a conservative, as orthodox in his ideas of success as he is enterprising in his efforts to succeed, while the nonconforming individualist is likely to treasure unconventional forms of self-expression and to regard the orthodoxy of the laissez-faire individualist as a threat to such self-expression and to novel ideas in general.

As these two types of individualists feud with one another, it is ironical that the ultimate accusation which each makes is that the other is betraying the community. Thus, while each in his own way places the individual before the group, each at the same time pays inverted tribute to the importance of the group by making the betrayal of the group the basis of his rejection of the other. To the nonconforming individualist the sin of the laissez-faire individualist is that he sacrifices the weak to the strong and that he values the opportunity for private advantage more than he values the general welfare. To the self-reliant individualist, the sin of the nonconforming individualist is that he denies the community the means of protecting its values and the morale of its members against injury by hostile or irresponsible persons or groups. His concept of the right of dissent is so absolute that he extends it not only to responsible critics who want to improve the society, but also to enemies who want to destroy it and to exploiters who are alert to every chance for arousing and playing upon the anxieties, the lusts, and the sadistic impulses which society, from the beginning of time, has struggled to control.

But before looking further at the relationship of these two modes of individualism to one another, let us first look at the historical context of the two. The individualism of self-reliance was essentially the response or adaptation of a people who had an undeveloped continent in front of them and who lacked institutional or technological devices for conquering it. Society needed persons who are what we call self-starters, persons who would go ahead and tackle the wilderness without waiting for signals to be given or for arrangements that would make it easy. It needed qualities of initiative and of ruggedness. It needed the attitude of Stonewall Jackson when he said that he would care for his own wounded and bury his own dead. In the conditions of pioneer America, where the services of the police and the church and the school and the hospital and the specialized economic occupations were often not available, it needed a man who could tote his own gun, pray his own prayers, and learn to read, write, and cipher by the light of a pine-knot fire. Andrew Jackson's mother is said to have admonished him at the parental knee, "Andy, never sue nobody. Always settle them matters yourself."

America needed a breed of men who would swarm over a wilderness which was a continent wide, and it produced the adaptation that was needed—the frontier American, famous in song and story as well as in the classic formulations of Frederick Jackson Turner. He was, it appears, rugged; he was self-reliant; he seems to have been magnificently successful; and he did tame the continent in record time—with the important aid, it must be added, of a tremendously effective new technology of power and machines. But was his self-reliance individualism? And, insofar as it was individualism, what were the social costs of developing this kind of individualism to such a pronounced degree? These questions are somewhat harder to answer.

Turner himself suggested that the frontier experience stimulated innovation, which of course means a break with conformity, a break with the past. He offered the hypothesis, which research has failed to vindicate, that the frontiersmen showed great fertility in working out new and untraditional political devices for the governments of their new states. But in fact, the tendency to imitate and copy the older political models was high. Professor Walter P. Webb has made a considerably more tenable argument that the men of the Great Plains seized upon certain technological innovations: the six-shooter, barbed wire, and the windmill. But this seems more a matter of physical adaptation than of a capacity for independent or deviant thought. The status of the frontiersman as an independent thinker is questionable indeed. Perhaps, one might add, it is unfair even to expect of him that he should have been an independent thinker. The physical demands upon him were very rigid, and rigid demands necessarily require one specific response, thus limiting the range or spectrum or variety of response. Nonconformity and diversity in attitude will flourish where the demands of the physical environment are not so harshly rigorous, and where they leave more latitude for variation from man to man. Nonconformity implies the possibility of varied reactions to the same situation; but the frontier, with its rigorous conditions of life, was too exacting in its demands to allow much choice for the frontiersman in the mode of his reaction.

In the past generation we have come to see, with increasing clarity, that the individualism of the American frontier was an individualism of personal self-reliance and of hardihood and stamina rather than an individualism of intellectual independence and personal self-expression. Arthur Schlesinger, Jr., for instance, has argued, I think convincingly, that the frontier was slow to perceive the problems arising in connection with the application of democracy to an industrial society and slow to develop social ideas of reform, so that these ideas, in fact, developed predominantly in the cities. At the same time when we were recognizing this, we were also beginning to count the social costs of the individualism of self-reliance, so that there has grown up a tendency to doubt whether the frontier influence was altogether a beneficial one in American life. As far back as Alexis de Tocqueville, we were warned in the clearest possible terms that American equality, which is peculiarly identified with the frontier, was conducive to conformity rather than to freedom, since it places the stigma of arrogance upon any man who ventures to set his personal judgment against the judgment of a majority of his equals. Arthur K. Moore, in his study of the frontier mind as exemplified in the backwoodsmen of Kentucky, has shown how readily the practicality of the frontier took the form of a blighting anti-intellectualism.[3] Many writers have begun to say that the frontiersman was spiritually and culturally impoverished by his isolation and by his predilection for a society in which the ties of community life were so weakened that he ceased to be, in any adequate sense, a social being. One who has stated this most strikingly, and perhaps in the most controversial

[3] Arthur K. Moore, *The Frontier Mind* (Lexington: University of Kentucky Press, 1957).

way, is Leslie Fiedler with his famous (or, as some citizens of Montana would say, infamous) comments on his earliest impressions of the people of that frontier state. Upon his arrival in Montana, says Fiedler:

I was met unexpectedly by the Montana Face. What I had been expecting, I do not clearly know; zest, I suppose, naiveté, a ruddy and straight-forward kind of vigor—perhaps even honest brutality. What I found seemed, at first glance, reticent, sullen, weary—full of self-sufficient stupidity; a little later it appeared simply inarticulate, with all the dumb pathos of what cannot declare itself; a face developed not for sociability or feeling, but for facing into the weather. It said friendly things to be sure, and meant them; but it had no adequate physical expressions even for friendliness, and the muscles around the mouth and eyes were obviously unprepared to cope with the demands of any more complicated emotion. I felt a kind of innocence behind it, but an innocence difficult to distinguish from simple ignorance. In a way there was something heartening in dealing with people who had never seen, for instance, a Negro or a Jew or a servant, and were immune to all their bitter meanings; but the same people, I knew, had never seen an art museum or a ballet or even a movie in any language but their own, and the poverty of experience had left the possibilities of the human face in them completely unrealized.[4]

Here, in effect, is the assertion that society had to pay too high a price for frontier individualism—that men as a group were penalized for the freedom of men as separate beings, and, in short, that individualism is not justified if it serves only individuals. It must serve society. Our conviction that it must is why we have never had any elite individualism that amounted to anything, and is also a striking commentary upon the paradoxical elements in the fact that we are committed to individualism at all.

Along with frontier individualism, the nineteenth century also

[4] Leslie A. Fiedler, *An End of Innocence* (Boston: The Beacon Press, 1955), pp. 134–135. Courtesy also of the *Kenyon Review*.

subscribed to the economic individualism of *laissez faire*. The two shared a great deal in common. Both exalted strength and stamina and scorned weakness or lack of practicality. Both enjoined the individual to fight for his own aspirations first and to subordinate consideration for the group to consideration for the enterpriser acting alone. Both made a virtue of independence but their independence meant a self-propelled drive toward the goals which society had prescribed rather than any real independence of mind in setting the goals for which to strive. Both were individualistic in a sense—certainly in the sense of "rugged individualism"—but it was an individualism that was more conservative than liberal, more hostile to dissent than favorable toward it.

It is a notable fact about laissez-faire individualism, however, that while it exalted the virtues of unregimented, uncontrolled, independent action by man acting alone, it never for a moment contended that the success of the unusual individual was more important than the welfare of the community. Instead, it constantly stressed the idea that the bold enterpriser served the community by daring to undertake projects which the community needed but which the rank and file were too unimaginative to initiate. The argument was much like that of the modern nonconforming individualist who defends dissenters not on the ground that the dissenter matters and that the conventional thinkers from whom he dissents do not, but that the community needs ideas which the conventional or orthodox thinkers cannot supply.

There is no need for me to recite here the elaborate arguments which Adam Smith stated so ingeniously, and which nineteenth-century publicists so dearly loved to repeat, that a providentially designed economic system (the unseen hand of God at work) took the selfish impulses and selfish actions of individuals and translated them into results which served the welfare of the community. This concept that the antagonistic rivalries of selfish and competing producers would create an optimum relationship between the social need for goods and the economic supply of goods is not only a subtle and by no means preposterous economic theory. It is also a renewed testimony that even the ardent individualists of the nineteenth century were not willing to base their faith in individualism upon any concept of the primacy of the interests of the individual over the interests of the group. Instead they made the interests of the group—that is, the society—the ground for their insistence that society must not be deprived of the contribution which the independent-minded individual can make.

During the Great Depression, a great many Americans grew to doubt that laissez-faire individualism really did serve the interests of the whole society. Our government under the New Deal abandoned it, and though we have had a span of a quarter of a century since that time, with two Republican administrations in the interim, there is no indication that we will return to the old faith in self-reliance and private action. Richard Hofstadter has subtitled his essay on Herbert Hoover "The Last Stand of Rugged Individualism," and there are probably not many, even among the conservatives, who would quarrel very much with this verdict.

In saying that the individualism of self-reliance has passed its high tide, I don't mean to suggest by any means that it has disappeared, or even that it does not remain, in some forms, a very dominant American attitude. Anyone who thinks that it is becoming extinct might well ponder over an analysis which Martha Wolfenstein and Nathan Leites made only a few years ago of the plots of a year's crop of American motion pictures of the A grade.

The major plot configuration in American films [they wrote] contrasts with both the British and the French. Winning is terrifically important and always possible though it may be a tough fight. The conflict is not an internal one [as in Hamlet]; it is not our own impulses which endanger us nor our own scruples that stand in our way. The hazards are all external, but they are not rooted in the nature of life itself. They are the hazards of a particular situation with which we find ourselves confronted. The hero is typically in a strange town where there are apt to be dangerous men and women of ambiguous character and where the forces of law and order are not to be relied on. If he sizes up the situation correctly, if he does not go off half-cocked but is still able to beat the other fellow to the punch once he is sure who the enemy is, if he relies on no one but himself, if he demands sufficient evidence of virtue from the girl, he will emerge triumphant. He will defeat the dangerous men, get the right girl, and show the authorities what's what.[5]

We all know that American boys, from the early years of childhood, are taught to stand up and fight back. Margaret Mead, incidentally, has commented cogently on this point.[6] So long as this is true, and so long as the self-reliant protagonist in the movie gets the desirable girl, it would be premature indeed to suggest that all the bark has been rubbed off the tradition of individualism in its rugged form. But certainly the tradition has come under attack and certainly it is, as we might say, selling at at a discount.

Now what is the basis of our discontent with the tradition of self-reliance? This is certainly a complex and difficult question, to which it may be brash to venture a simple answer, but in many respects it appears that the point of the criticism is that stress on self-reliance was carried to a point where it emphasized private goals and private values too much at the cost of community

[5] Martha Wolfenstein and Nathan Leites, *Movies: A Psychological Study* (Glencoe, Illinois: Free Press, 1950), p. 298.

[6] Margaret Mead, *And Keep Your Powder Dry: An Anthropologist Looks at America* (New York: William Morrow & Company, Inc., 1942), p. 141.

goals and community values. The coherence of the community was impaired, the vitality of the community was lowered. Leslie Fiedler's men with the Montana face are essentially men who have been starved of the psychological nourishment which community life could offer.

This criticism can be detected, I think, in quite a number of different forms. For instance, Stanley Elkins, in his comparison of slavery in North America and in South America, comments on the fact that in South America certain community institutions such as the church and the government were strong enough to assert a concern for the slave, and to stand, as it were, in certain respects, between the slave and his master.[7] But in North America, the naked authority of the master was tempered in hardly any way by the institutional force of the community. This amounts to saying that private values had eclipsed public values in the United States. Many other writers have expressed concern about the lack of corporate *esprit* among Americans, and some of the concern about the lack of reciprocal support for one another among American prisoners of war in Korea, as contrasted, for instance, with that among Turkish prisoners of war, was also addressed to the fear that we have emphasized private values, or what may be called privatism, too much and community values not enough. The old Yankee prayer:

> God save me and my wife,
> My son John and his wife,
> Us four and no more

may have expressed an attitude that was rooted too deep for comfort.

Many of the comments that we have had on privatism as an unfortunate dimension of American individualism have been ex-

[7] Stanley M. Elkins, *Slavery: A Problem in American Institutional and Intellectual Life* (Chicago: University of Chicago Press, 1959), pp. 27–80.

pressed in strong and somewhat controversial terms, but Gabriel Almond, in his *The American People and Foreign Policy,* gave us what might be regarded as a sober and measured statement of this point.

The American, [said Almond] is primarily concerned with "private values," as distinguished from social-group, political, or religious-moral values. His concern with private, worldly success is his most absorbing aim. In this regard it may be suggested by way of hypothesis that in other cultures there is a greater stress on corporate loyalties and values and a greater personal involvement with political issues or with other-worldly religious values.[8]

With the twentieth century, as I have already tried to suggest, American individualism took on a new emphasis. The frontier was disappearing, and *laissez faire* was having its wings clipped. According to a well-known phrase which is perhaps a trifle too pat, human rights were replacing property rights. The new expounders of the American tradition re-examined the sacred documents and concluded that the priceless feature of our heritage was the principle of nonconformity, or dissent. Of course, they had perfectly sound historical grounds for tracing the principle of dissent far back in American history. Puritanism itself was a fairly radical form of dissent, as well as a harsh system for enforcing conformity. Ralph W. Emerson, that great apostle of individualism, had not only exalted self-reliance; he had exalted dissent also. "Whoso would be a man," Emerson said, "must be a non-conformist." In our own day, the sanction which we give to dissent is suggested quite clearly in the antithesis which we constantly set up of liberty versus authority and of self-expression versus conformity.

The exponents of this new kind of individualism went forward

[8] Gabriel A. Almond, *The American People and Foreign Policy* (New York: Harcourt, Brace and Company, Inc., 1950), p. 48.

rejoicing, for quite some time, that individualism was now purged of the taints of privatism and of conformity. For the spokesmen of the individualism of nonconformity were very often men who could in no sense be accused of indifference to the interests of the group, of society. Most of them are what we call liberals—using the term with a fairly clear understanding of what kind of people we mean, even if we cannot quite define their exact quality—and the liberals were so concerned with the welfare of the group that they often gave it a priority over the rights of the individual. Their opponents offered an implicit recognition to this fact by angrily denouncing them as "collectivists." How could a man whose fault, if he has one, is that he is too collectivist—too group-minded—legitimately be accused of privatism? How could a man who supports the American Civil Liberties Union and consistently *épaters* the bourgeoise be suspected of conformity? The new individualism, then, was an emancipated individualism, cleansed of its old, middle-class sins of privatism and of conformity.

Yet before we accept the conclusion that the nineteenth-century doctrine of Progress has been vindicated again, and that individualism has reached a new and perfected condition, it may be worthwhile to apply one of the weapons of dissent, the weapon of skepticism, and to ask in a truly searching way whether conformity and privatism are really dead, whether true self-expression has come into its own at last, or whether, to some extent, conformity and privatism have merely found new modes of expression.

To pursue this question, as it relates to conformity, one would have to ask whether we have ceased to follow the crowd, or whether we have to some extent merely changed the crowd which we follow? Have we ceased to be cultists, or have we primarily changed our cults? Does the liberal who makes a fetish of his nonconformity actually show much more readiness to get out of step with his fellow liberals than does the avowedly conformist conservative with his fellow conservatives?

Stated a little differently and a little more abstractly, conformity is the faithful, unquestioning compliance with the standards imposed by a group. But to say this is to say that whether you call a man a conformist or a dissenter is very often not a question of his intrinsic independence, but a question of what group you measure him by. A Communist, for instance, measured by the reference group of the American public, is a dissenter and a nonconformist, but measured by the reference group of his own adoption, the Communist group, he is the supreme conformist— more so than a Baptist or a Rotarian, for he has completely abdicated his capacity to judge questions on their own merits and has embraced, *verbatim ac litteratim,* a whole body of doctrine which, like medieval theology, has answered all questions before they arise.

David Riesman has dealt with this point with sharp perception in his essay "The Saving Remnant," where he says, "The Bohemians and rebels are not usually autonomous; on the contrary, they are zealously tuned in to the signals of a defiant group that finds the meaning of life in a compulsive nonconformity to the majority group."[9] In an extraordinarily acute article called "The Bored and the Violent," Arthur Miller has discussed this point in connection with extreme manifestations of sadistic violence among juvenile delinquents. Miller makes the striking point that, among these youths, who are responding to society by defiance in its most extreme form, the real pattern is not one of deviation but of conformity—a blind, abject conformity to the expectations of their peers. As Miller says, "The delinquent, far from being

---

[9] Riesman, *Individualism Reconsidered,* p. 117.

the rebel, is the conformist par excellence. He is actually incapable of doing anything alone."[10] His reliance upon his gang is, of course, the measure of this lack of capability. Here, one is reminded of a cartoon in the *New Yorker* some time ago showing a young woman, attractive and appearing very much an average American girl, speaking somewhat crossly to her husband, who was dressed in the prescribed uniform of a beatnik. Her question to him was, "Why do you have to be a nonconformist like everyone else?"

If there is any group in our society which makes a truly earnest effort to cultivate real intellectual freedom and fearless inquiry, it is no doubt the academic and intellectual community. Yet even here, do we not have a certain incidence of what might be called academic conformity? Would not an academic who in 1960 spoke out loud and clear for Richard Nixon have shocked the sense of propriety of a gathering of academics as much as an overt glorification of the New Frontier would shock a group of investment bankers? Do not even the academics have their orthodoxies and their conventions? Do not these conventions require that in the case of a novelist, for example, he make a conforming obeisance to nonconformity by following the practice of employing as frequently as possible the monosyllabic words for the functions of sex and bodily elimination which have now become almost trite but which still have a gratifying capacity to startle a good many readers and to attract a good many buyers who hope to be startled? And do not the conventions also require that the book reviewer also conform and prove that he too is an emancipated spirit by dutifully praising the fearless realism of the author without reference to whether his work has merit?

One more illustration may be in order here—the case of an

[10] Arthur Miller, "The Bored and the Violent," *Harper's Mgaazine* (November, 1962), pp. 51–52.

academic of irreproachable standing. When Hannah Arendt published an article questioning whether the integration of public schools ought to be attempted by the exercise of public authority, the result was not, as one might have hoped, a rough-and-tumble scrimmage between her and persons who disagreed with her. It was rather a shocked silence, a polite looking in the other direction as if no one had noticed. It was, indeed, the same reaction as if she had belched in church. Miss Arendt had questioned a point on which liberals have established a dogma to which they require conformity, and they were shocked in a prudish way to hear this dogma questioned.

If there is some question about the completeness of the triumph of nonconformity, there is perhaps also a question concerning the finality of the victory over privatism. Surely the shaggy, long-haired, or rugged breed of individualism is gone for good, and we will no longer sacrifice the interests of society to the individualism of *laissez faire*. But can any generation, even our own, completely reconcile the social needs of the group with other personal needs of the individual? And must we not expect that even the new style of defense of individual right will sometimes be conducted at the expense of what might best serve society as a whole? The new individualism firmly repudiates all the nineteenth-century freebooters who used to exploit the public economically, but it still thinks, and perhaps ought to think, in terms of man as separate rather than of man in the group. Thus, when it is confronted with what we call crime—the large-scale incidence of violence in our society—it seems more concerned with the rehabilitation of the deviant individual who has committed the violence than with safeguarding those anonymous persons upon whom the violence is committed. When confronted with the sale in every drugstore of magazines which exploit sex, it does not really ask whether it would be better for society if the drugstores did not purvey this material. It does not ask whether the publisher who makes a fast buck by this shoddy commercial enterprise is different from a patent-medicine manufacturer who also makes a fast buck by selling nostrums but is regulated, hopefully, by the Pure Food and Drug Act. It asks instead who will dare to violate freedom of the press in maintaining an informed public opinion.

Perhaps this is the right question to ask. I would hesitate to say that it is clearly wrong. But what I do venture to suggest is that the freedom of the individual, in relation to his society, cannot be absolute, basically because the individual and the society are not really separate. The individual acquires his full identity only as a member of society, and society itself is, in the last analysis, a multiplicity of individuals. The American tradition, which rejected elite individualism from the beginning, has always shown enough concern for the social values to seek to justify its individualism—whether self-reliant or nonconformist —in social terms. Thus the competitive system in economics was defended not on the ground of the great profits which it would bring to some individuals, but with the claim that it would assure economic vigor for the society. Similarly, the sanctions which have surrounded dissent were based less upon approval of the dissenter than upon the need of society for an unrestricted "free trade in ideas." Moreover, each school of individualism cared enough for social values to attack the other for betraying them. Thus the dissentients accused the self-reliants of sacrificing the weak to the strong and the community to its predatory members, while the self-reliants accused the dissentients of sacrificing the strong to the weak and the community to its aberrant members. Perhaps both accusations have been justified, for both groups have remained primarily committed to a strong individualistic emphasis, and in the long struggle between two schools of individualism, the values of the community have often lacked effective defenders on either side. Neither form of individualism has had enough genuine concern for real group values, shared community values, to hold a proper balance between the centrifugal and the centripetal forces.

Neither one has been willing to recognize that the tension between the individual and the group can never be treated as a simple antithesis, involving a simple choice. For each, in its logically pure form, contains implications which are unacceptable to most of us. The emphasis on the individual essentially implies a component of privatism which would sacrifice the interests of the group to the interests of a limited number of its members, and this implication is not acceptable in the long run to a democratic society; the emphasis on the group implies the subordination of the qualities of the mind and spirit of man, standing by himself, to the pressures of men in a herd, and this implication, too, is unacceptable to a people who believe that society exists for man and not man for society. Therefore, we can never make a clearcut, exclusive choice in favor of either individualism, as it is called, or collectivism, as it is called. While philosophers are engaged in pursuing one or the other of these two to their logical extremes and even their logical absurdities, people in everyday life will go on, trying in the future, as they have tried in the past, to accommodate these two and imperfectly to reconcile the indispensable values which are inherent in them both. As Riesman stated it, "Such terms as 'society' and 'individual' tend to pose a false, as well as a shifting dichotomy."

◇◇

Dogmatic[1] Innocence
Self-Assertion in Modern American Literature

FREDERICK J. HOFFMAN

SURELY NO AMERICAN CITIZEN, of whatever political allegiance, will publicly doubt that individualism (as opposed to conformism or organizational timidity) is a desirable human condition. My object here, therefore, is mainly descriptive rather than prescriptive. Indeed, individualism, or self-assertion, or the ego's right of independence from excessive pressures of the "other," is so firmly entrenched as a privilege and a characteristic of American society that one would as soon attack motherhood, or ask Dr. Spock to write a handbook for homosexuals, as deny it. The "real, right question" before this symposium has to do not so much with the fact of individualism as with its mutations of be-

---

[1] I use the word "dogmatic," as I think I explain sufficiently in the paper, in a double sense: as expressing the strength of will involved in expressing the right to innocence; but also in the religious sense: that is, that it is a significant fact of American belief that the self must be preserved in its "purity" at all costs. For the analogy with theological "dogmatics," see *A Handbook of Christian Theology* (Cleveland, Ohio: World Publishing Company [Meridian Books], 1958), pp. 80–85.

ing and definition in our century. My task is to see if literature helps to illuminate the discussion.

Let me suggest at first two major historical sources of American individualism: the inward-looking Puritan theoanalysis of the seventeenth century, the two emotional extremes of which reached an explosive climax in Jonathan Edwards of the eighteenth; and the metaphors of the self experimented with and exploited by Ralph Waldo Emerson and other Transcendentalists. Elaboration of these suggestions would more than take the time allotted me in this session. But I should wish to say that both puritanism and transcendentalism imposed stresses and strains upon self-assertion in twentieth-century American literature: the scrupulous analysis of human action characteristic of puritanism caused a strange mixture of self-concern and socioreligious scrutiny of conduct and human worth; the metaphors used in Emerson's essay "Nature" and elsewhere bespoke a confidence in the self that made the idea of a superintending God almost superfluous to the act of self-analysis.

To elaborate upon these ideas is to risk the appearance at least of a series of inflated half-truths. But I should like to suggest that the crisis of individualism in nineteenth-century American thought comes not in the struggle of naturalists against critical gentility, or in the fight against social taboos that seems so characteristic of the early twentieth-century milieu, but in the strange paradoxes encountered by men of rational good will whose researches into the facts of human consciousness seemed to collapse their desire to "believe" in accepted moral and theological principles. That is, the puritan scrutiny of the self in its presumedly continuous life led to a scientific, a rational, analysis of self as consciousness.

I think the major turning point in this history is William James's superbly detailed, yet suspiciously naïve, analysis of con sciousness in his *Principles of Psychology* (1890). Searching for a definition of "self," James there had to conclude that the self is not substantively tenable but is only a *process* of experiencing. He therefore anticipated, in his own special, indigenously well-intentioned American way, the melodrama of Jean-Paul Sartre's description of choice, freedom, and responsibility. There is a curious, even a sentimentally interesting, aspect of James's voyage of psychological discovery. I see James as an affecting and fascinating example of the Victorian scientist whose intense concern for verifiable truth leads him away from the convictions he would prefer to hold and lands him in a distressing situation from which he hopes to *will* his escape. He is, therefore, the antecedent of the twentieth-century romantic who, not able wholly to deny scientific conclusions, nevertheless cannot bring himself to accept them, so *wills* his denial of them. In short, the evidence that there is no substantial self (no "soul," no Emersonian creative epi-center from which the world is "realized"), but only moments or instants of consciousness, is an intolerable discovery. So James relies upon Victorian reassurances, but most of all upon a Victorian-democratic definition of the will. It is one thing to argue that immortality is a fact and not just a vain hope (James's *Human Immortality*, 1898), as James did in late years, in public lectures and in letters to his sister Alice. But this argument is an act of desperation; the major concern is to restore to the self the possibilities that it may guarantee its continuity in time, that such a continuance of conscious being is a supreme responsibility (a "dreadful freedom," as the existentialists put it) of a conative being.[2]

---

[2] For a more detailed discussion of all of these points, see my essays: "Freedom and Conscious Form," *Virginia Quarterly Review*, 37 (Spring, 1961); and "William James and the Modern Literary Consciousness," *Criticism*, 4 (Winter, 1962).

The core of any discussion of twentieth-century individualism must account for this drama: the struggle of the will against increasing evidence of both a closed society and a closed psychology. In the early years of the century—which were really not the twentieth century at all but an extension of the nineteenth—it was possible to conceive of social action as a means of guaranteeing or expressing self-reliance. Hence such books as Upton Sinclair's *The Jungle* (1906) and Lincoln Steffens' *The Shame of the Cities* (1904) seemed to have a bearing upon the question. In fact, social reform served more as a substitute for self-analysis than an extension of it. It is true that this is the conventional, the "historical," expression of individualism. Notable instances of American history involve the public hero who opposes the conventional and the acceptable but wins through in one way or another. I do not think that twentieth-century literature offers many examples of such heroism.

The major expressions of the will in early twentieth-century literature are desperate assertions of the "dogma" of the self against what appear to be overwhelming evidences denying its autonomy. While the work of most American writers at the turn of the century seems now to be terribly naïve, it exhibits several striking variants of the dilemma I have discussed in William James's case. The great bogey of naturalism was that of an extra-personal "force," unearthed as a consequence of scientific diligence, which put the self entirely at its disposal and rendered it almost entirely helpless. The naturalist melodrama was often divided evenly between the hero's realization that he could do nothing to help himself and the author's distress that he had created so helpless a being.

Against this repetitive description of human helplessness are posed several kinds of self-assertion. These latter tend primarily to defend or to preserve the dogma of self, the powerful and almost unshakable conviction of the Emersonian romantic will, that the self does substantively exist and that it does have at least a partial creative control over its own destiny. I think it important that these be considered forms of self-assertion; they do not emerge logically or correctly from any prior analysis of the self in society but are expressions of the romantic "will to be." Implicit in each of them are the writer's prior assumptions concerning what the self is and what its circumstances should properly be. But superintending all these assumptions is the major one that the human self not only exists but that circumstances of personal and social dignity require that it exist. I can see no other explanation of E. A. Robinson's vigorous assertions of the self as a being related to some superluminary or Logos, despite the parade of circumstantial ironies which affect the creatures of his Tilbury Town. Ultimately we exist and propagate our kind, he says in *The Man Against the Sky*, because we "do" and because we "must"; we should not, were it not well that we should. This assertion is a form of the romantic will, a descendant of Emerson's, that culminates in a kind of philosophical therapy by a process of negating a negation. The sense of doing because we must is one of the terrible consequences of an individualism that does not profit from serious consideration of the responsibilities involved. We may always say, "Why must we?" do one thing or another. But this kind of challenge is not really convincing. The ambiguities of the American self are the direct result of feeling that we "must" and the counteracting suspicion that we "really ought not."

The First World War must be considered a major, and in some respects, a traumatic, experience in the twentieth-century history of the American dogma of self. This is true not only because of the War's violence, the first real experience of violence in a half

century, but because it was the beginning of an organized national will (as distinguished from an autonomous will) which
has become a major characteristic of twentieth-century America.
In American society as a whole, the drift since 1918 has been
away from the Emersonian world and toward an organizational
condition which thwarts and deprives the individual self, and
drives it to a condition of despair.

The literature of the 1920s is important in the fact of its being
a final expression of the nineteenth-century self against the enor-
mities of control and arbitrary restrictiveness of which World
War I was the climax. It is also a remarkable literature in the
general conviction it seems to demonstrate of the hope that the
virtues of style and intelligence, if they cannot conquer suppres-
sive forces, at least may be thought superior to them.

This latter point is uniquely important in the history of individualism in twentieth-century literature. It is closely related to
the condition of fragmentation and isolation suffered as a consequence of the discovery of "self as process" in James's *Principles
of Psychology*. The fact is that the literature of the 1920s is a re-
statement of this discovery. The major activity of this literature
consists of experiment in forms and the examination of the object
(as object) in depth. It is not a new event in American literature,
though it is an exceptional one. Note how frequently the modern
self (the word "soul" is almost invariably ridiculed) is seen
fragmentarily in an oxymoronic focus. It is imaged forth, pre-
sented evocatively rather than melodramatically. Gertrude Stein's
attempts to present a static self, or a self moving slowly in terms
of vagrant and tenuous variations upon a few essential traits,
form a transitional effort from William James's explorations to
the imagistic-oriented literature of the 1920s.

This move toward the "corner view" of the self is significantly
related to a postwar antinomian view, a distrust of the general-

ities that go with, or sustain, social structures and a trust in separate individual definitions of self. Hemingway's attempt to communicate the War in a handful of brief "dispatches" is symptomatic. So too, his representation of character and action in isolation from "normal society" is related to the isolation of self from large social framework or generality. Hemingway's heroes move on the margins of convention and improvise their own means of adapting to a world known only in terms of the immediate present. Except that they must be analyzed as victims of it, they are outside history; and they must move in terms of a fragmented world which exists only as it comes within range of the consciousness of the narrator-hero.

I am trying to emphasize that the literature of the 1920s was a remarkably varied set of stylistic and structural improvisations. Half of these were attempts to come to terms with the idea of the self as process, as existing within the immediacy of a present scene and cut off from a significant past or a predictable future. The image, the scene, the narrative move from fragment to variant of experience, and they are all instruments in the description of self as process. But there is also a literature of assertion that is, if not antithetically opposed to, at least different from the improvisational perspectives upon experience I've been describing. Once again, the assertion, like that of Robinson's *The Man Against the Sky*, is impulsive, defensive, and apologetic. It is linked to the earlier history of Mallarméan *symbolisme*, one of whose tenets is that the "word" has a mystic value to which the subtle instruments of art ultimately aspire. This is a form of absolute trust in the agencies of, as distinguished from the fact of, assertion. Yet, in its American expressions it is hedging and doubtful. One of the major traits of American self-assertion is that there is always something of what Kenneth Burke calls "comic self-consciousness" involved in it. In the most remarkable example of this literature, Hart Crane's "The Bridge" (1930), there are occasions when the large transcendent assertions of the first and last poems in the sequence are hedged by doubt, even by a comic remorse; and penultimately, just before Crane tries to affirm the strength of an absolute belief, his hero undergoes a distressing failure of confidence. Quite aside from these evidences, there is the figure of Crane's protagonist: he is the "poet," the "bedlamite," the companion of Rip Van Winkle and of the thousand hoboes who dot the land's immensities. So that, even in this literary expression of the romantic will, there is a semicomic reserve, like that of Baudelaire's clowns, or *chiffonniers*, or Laforgue's Hamlets and Pierrots, or Rouault's lords, Christs, and clowns.

The remarkable fact about the literature of the 1920s is the absence of ideological absolutes in the decade. I don't mean that there weren't ideological saints and sinners, but simply that these were not very important. No significant writer in the decade attended to social structures from an ideological bias. If there is a dogma in the decade, it is that of dogmatic innocence, as that was defined in the basic terms of Emersonian romanticism; to it was added the dogma of style, the most extreme version of which is the mysticism of the word.

This condition was radically altered in the 1930s, a decade in which ideology was stringently applied to a majority of serious literary works. The 1930s were a period of intellectual crisis. The American dogma of egocentric innocence was repeatedly threatened by strategies of a closed frame of social interpretation. I should contend that such a manipulation of literature is inimical to it. In any case, while the 1930s are immensely interesting to the sociologist, the intellectual historian, and the political scientist, they were not characteristically or traditionally American; the historical dogma of self-definition was threatened by the danger of being closed off by narrowly ideological meanings. Writers in the decade also suffered from a naïveté, or a too ready willingness to accept quick definitions.

The majority of them did, that is. It was an uncomfortable intellectual world for the most part. But if its literature was oppressed by social absolutes, there were ways of assimilating them to the native tradition. Nothing is so sentimentally "patriotic," for example, as the lone struggle of Ma Joad and what is left of her family to reassert and to defend the virtues of the Emersonian self. The "lesson" that "the people" will live on somehow because Ma Joad will show them the way, is a none too subtle subversion of the Emersonian praise of the self and of Thoreau's projection of the self into geographical and metaphysical distances. In other words, no ideology can contain the Joads; their struggle must be motivated by a trust in the power of the self to project beyond ego center into society. It is a sentimental extension of dogmatic innocence, to suit the far-reaching necessities of a political, an ideological decade.

Least affected by ideological persuasions were the most talented writers of the South, who were responsible for the most distinguished literature of the decade. There is no simple way of discussing the work of William Faulkner, for example; yet his is the most profound and the least constricted examination of the human condition in the decade, perhaps in the century. Nevertheless, the strong pedagogic tone in Faulkner's work, which overtly showed itself only in the last years of his life, was implicitly there from the start. The principal contribution Faulkner made—to the subject of this discussion at least—lay in the examination of consciousness, or in the examination of human phenomena through the several perspectives of consciousness that he used both as a means of narration and indirectly as an examination of moral issues and human substance.

Faulkner's novels contain scores of human types, each of whom in some way or other fights against the denial of the substantial self. His basic defense of the human moral substance is not God or Christ (who exist as metaphors "to be used in the novels") but "the verities" which he defined and defended in his Stockholm address. Put simply and baldly as he put them there, these verities have no more real substance than the warm glow of comfort the reader gets from Ma Joad's determination to "go on" because "we owe it to the people" who "will endure" because they've been made to endure. But in his best work of the 1930s, Faulkner had not yet been stricken by the evangelical virus and was able to define his meanings without subtracting from his art.

I should say, by way of recapitulation, that American literature of our century (1) suffered from the blight of naturalism but asserted and affirmed beyond its apparently logical conclusions; (2) in the postwar world enjoyed an extreme freedom of intellectual and stylistic improvisation, on the assumption that each man's insights were, *sui generis*, valuable and important; and (3) in the 1930s gave in at least part way to ideological pressures which had least to offer the American dogma of the self and threatened it the most.

Ihab Hassan, in one of the most stimulating books of the past decade, speaks of "radical innocence"; he means an affirmation of the romantic will, a "radical" assertion of self-importance in the face of a frightening testimony of human futility.[3] My phrase, dogmatic innocence, involves me in much the same view, though it has the additional suggestion (through the ambiguous meaning of "dogmatic") of a radical and powerful reassertion, a romantically willed continuance of central American dogmas.

[3] Ihab Hassan, *Radical Innocence: The Contemporary American Novel* (Princeton: Princeton University Press, 1961). See especially Part I.

Let me try to explain. Emerson's view of the self as a creative center, the Swedenborgian and Fourieriste notions of the human self symbolically collaborating with the soul of God to aid in the completion of both: these seem to me to be the root sources of certain essential dogmas in American history—truths or affirmations that are expounded and applied and illustrated as the conditions require. One should note from the beginning that these views are irrational, that they are willed and become articles of belief only through an act of the will. I suppose that this is true of all questions of belief: the will to believe is either strong enough to encourage heroic exercises of the imagination, or is so feeble as to make all expressions of the will difficult to accept.

Mr. Hassan has pointed out that the radical innocence of his subject is a willed and a strong expression of a perdurable human power in the face of discouraging evidences to the contrary. I should want merely to add that the dogmatics (that is, the articles of faith) of this innocence have a history that reaches into the beginnings of American literature and thought.

The facts recur with especial vigor when one contemplates the literature of the past ten years. If one excepts the O'Haras and Richters and the others who write on order and according to formula (John Steinbeck is surely not very far above them), the great literature of this generation comes from the deprived, the minority, the "marginal" groups; each has had its embarrassing and distressing experience of being deliberately ignored, and each has consciously exploited its minority status. I should list the principal contemporary American groups of writers as these: the Southern, the Northern Jewish (for the most part urban), the Negro, and (for want of a better term) the Beat. A common denominator is difficult to find; but I should say that all of them are closely acquainted with violence as a major quality of the contemporary milieu, that each of them defends the special characteristics of its status as a minority, that the lesson of either background or experience is often and cogently communicated in each case.

The surprising fact is that they are all marginal groups. Surely this deserves some explanation, in terms of the history of American respect for individualism. Is it that the strongest self-assertions always come from marginal personalities (hasn't the artist always been considered marginal in America)? Is there something peculiar about the contemporary condition that helps to explain? What, for example, would Emerson have had to say to William Burroughs, or Burroughs to him? A partial explanation is that the assertion of the American dogma of self presently requires a more violent expression of the will to self-persistence, and that this strength of will is to be found only in these marginal societies.

I do not deny the absurdities of some of the literature: the aimless rambling, the naïve assertions of enthusiasms based on small knowledge and less information, the stupidity of assuming that violence is in itself a virtue provided it is violent enough, the false nostalgia and envy concerning the qualities of a marginal class, etc. But, if one is being merely descriptive here for the moment, it is possible to say that a common concern animates and even dominates much of this literature: it is an existentialist concern, though it scarcely resembles the intricate analytics of a formal existentialist philosophy.

Let me suggest some of the existentialist characteristics: the sense of the probing question concerning the purpose of existence (that is, if I am I, then what significantly follows); the sense of being "in situation" (that is, the hero is in a place and of a condition of which he is aware; he is also in a sense the creator of the situation he is in, in that he has chosen to be in it); the feeling of being *engagé* (that is, the degree of his involvement is strong, and he is an initiator of the action which defines himself as a be-ing); the absence, or the scarcity, of moral, legal, or religious systems or codes that are not of his making (that is, he impro-vises the rationale of his being and of his continuing to exist).

I should say that the present conditions in which the self must be preserved are radically different from those of a generation, even a decade ago. There are no genuine ideologies to go to for comfort or solace. The atmosphere of the 1920s is not relevant, because its sense of freedom depended on a sure knowledge of victory over Victorian and nineteenth-century *bêtes noires*; the convenience of this scapegoat is no longer available. The dog-matics of present self-assertion are defined and pursued in an ex-istential circumstance. Notice that all but one of these groups is without a history (the exception is the Southern group, and even here it is a history of adjustment to defeat that lies behind the literature).

I should like to elaborate. The urban Jewish disposition, which is now perhaps the strongest of the groups I've mentioned, is based on two important facts of Jewish life: its sense of self-mocking wit and the absence of a clear idea of post-mortem re-wards and punishment (this latter fact forces the moral issue to the foreground of present, mortal, human existence in a way that is true of no other culture group). In other words, the Jewish situation is an existential one, within limits. The self-assertion in this circumstance is hedged by doubt, by a "comic self-consciousness," but ultimately the hero's decision is all but en-tirely his own; he has a tradition, but it demands that he act on his own initiative.

The Negro literature has come a long way from an awkward self-preoccupation to a view of the race that, even though it is still self-conscious, does at least make some literary virtue of its self-consciousness. The work of Ralph Ellison, for example, makes the same kind of imaginative capital of its subject as the work of Saul Bellow makes of its. Quite aside from the question whether white envy of the Negro disposition is too absurd to be taken seriously, there is the fact that the Negro condition offers brilliant illustrations of the self's suppression. James Baldwin is able to explore every aspect of that situation, in his novels as well as his nonfictional prose. There is a strength of assertion in this literature that is surely a supreme example of the romantic will in process of self-definition.

The Beat literature is more difficult to discuss because it is more varied and more diffuse and because there is more bad literature—more nonsense disguised as sense. But at its most powerful it is more intense, more savage, more inclusive in its use of the metaphors of willed marginality, than any of the others.

In another essay, I have tried to define the major "beat" situation in terms of these three metaphors:[4] On the Road (the vagabond theme in American literature here takes on a new meaning and the experience of being on the road is radically different from what it was in other times and situations) ; On the Edge (this is partly a spatial, partly a psychological metaphor; in its simplest sense it means "on the margins of society") ; and In the Box (that is, the physical circumstances of either willed or enforced imprisonment). The third of these, I might add, is significantly related to Poe's imagery of tombs, or tomblike dark structures ("with addled mosses dank"). The Beat literature at its most intense explores the implications of all three of these metaphors. Its major effect is not so much to describe the marginal life but to use it as weapon against the center, and it is in this respect closely related to the savagely effective work in the

[4] See my "Introduction" to *Marginal Manners* (Evanston, Illinois: Row, Peterson, 1962).

drama of Jean Genet, of Arthur Adamov, and of Edward Albee.

These literatures are all products of violence. There is much violence in them, but I should say that for the most part it is a violence of the romantic will attempting to break through the accumulated barriers to self-assertion. In many respects it echoes the violence of World War II. As the first World War forced Hemingway, temporarily at least, into stylistic discretions, World War II, and especially its climax in the atom bomb, seems mainly to have pushed the writer into extremes of violent self-assertion.

Perhaps the most revealing, and the most symptomatic, of recent self-assertions appeared in an essay by Norman Mailer, called "The White Negro" (*Dissent,* Summer 1957). Having provided the setting—the war, the "bomb," the collapse of convincing securities—Mailer speaks of the arrival of "the American existentialist," whom he calls the hipster:

> . . . the man who knows that if our collective condition is to live with instant death by atomic war, relatively quick death by the State as *l'univers concentrationnaire,* or with a slow death by conformity with every creative and rebellious instinct stifled . . . why then the only life-giving answer is to accept the terms of death, to live with death as immediate danger, to divorce oneself from society, to exist without roots, to set out on that uncharted journey into the rebellious imperatives of the self.

The deadly earnestness of this passage (its evangelical humorlessness), its use of imperatives, and the command to man that he must match the dreadfulness of life with a willed dreadfulness of his own—all of these traits suggest the extremes to which the Emersonian dogmatic innocence has been forced.

I should like to conclude with an attempt to place this discussion of American self-assertion in a larger context. I have suggested in another essay that there are three principal lines of descent in the modern view of the self:[5] that beginning with the speculations of Jean-Paul Sartre; that of Albert Camus's attempts to face and to adjust to the "world of the absurd"; and the semi-religious, semimundane speculations of Dostoevski in *Notes from Underground* and *The Idiot.* The brooding analytics of Sartre have had a pervasive influence, not the least in post-World War II America. The speculations of *Being and Nothingness* (1943) are an elaborate extension of James's *Principles of Psychology*: they provide not only a more detailed analysis of the epistemological self-center, but a more than adequate sketch of the melodrama of self-choice and self-continuance.

Camus moved in his career from a flat statement of "the absurd" to a point where human endurance, responsibility, and guilt became psychological "verities" and were on the way to becoming moral and metaphysical verities when Camus was accidentally killed in 1960. The importance of Camus lies outside philosophical speculation, and he is therefore closer to the character of American self-assertion. The Camusien hero becomes a model of forbearance and integrity; he is a superb example of the secular hero. It is not merely coincidental that Camus should have interested himself in Faulkner, who belongs to his later career as Hemingway is appropriate to the earlier. The heroes of Faulkner's last novels (*The Reivers* excepted) are not dissimilar from Camus's Dr. Rieux of *The Plague*; they are men who tolerate men's follies, help occasionally to commit them, and ultimately testify to a hard core of human self-reliance and endurance. How close the two men might have come had Camus not been cut off suddenly from his career it is difficult to say. The important point is that their positions mediate between

[5] "The Wheel of Self," *Journal of Existential Psychiatry*, 2 (Summer, 1961).

the extremes of psychological analysis and irrational, willful assertion.

The line of descent from Dostoevski is much more complex. It has two major directions: the introspective and speculative, on the one hand, and the apocalyptic or holistic. The first stems from the introspective broodings of *Notes from Underground*; there is a history in European literature that begins there, includes many minor Russian novelists, in twentieth-century literature picks up the tortured inner debates and self-accusations of Kafka's fiction, and includes the obsessively diligent concern with self-identity in Samuel Beckett's novels and plays. The other line of descent is closer to the irrational explosions of self-will I have noted in Beat or "hipster" literature. The European precedents are Dostoevski's Prince Myshkin (*The Idiot*) and Rimbaud's *voyant*, who achieves his state of surreal holistic vision by what Rimbaud called "un long et raisonné dérèglement de tous les sens."[6] It is important to notice that Rimbaud advises the *cultivation* of this "derangement of all the senses," just as the most vigorous of the Beat or "hip" writers force their self-identities upon others through extremes of physical strength or emotional hatred; the emphasis is on an attempt to achieve a pure condition of irrational status and feeling.

The key to this form of self-expression is intensity, whether in sexual domination or in the power to inflict pain—both extremes of the will to "murder and create" which Eliot's Prufrock so conspicuously lacked. There are savage, destructive humor (the "black bile" of William Burroughs' *Naked Lunch*, 1962), which goes far beyond the Swiftian contempt of humanity; the cultivation of passion as a test of self-identity, power, and finesse, as in

---

[6] In a famous letter to Paul Demeny, May 15, 1871.

Norman Mailer's recent work (fragments of which are offered in his *Advertisements for Myself,* 1959); and a more subdued, less vicious though surely not less candid expression of unconventional passion, as in the work of Henry Miller. Each of these forms of self-expression is an extreme of the willed protection of self-identity. The setting is war, violence, "the bomb"; the strategy is to exercise the privilege of a "radical innocence," in order to preserve the essential American dogma of the inviolability of the self.

It is perhaps significant enough that these marginal personalities are seldom taken seriously, though at least one psychiatric study of some of them has already been published, and I suspect many sociologists are looking at them eagerly, prepared to box them in with statistically tested and proved phrases and categories. I offer them here as a suggestion of what has happened in recent years to Emersonian dogmatics. To preserve the self, at least in the fullness of confidence which Emerson gave it, it is necessary to split society into fragments of convention and marginality. Much of the energy and passion and some at least of the intelligence lie with the latter. In any case, the present existence of so strong (and often so talented) a marginal society testifies to the strength of these dogmas: that the self is and must be strong enough to stand up to and against society, and that the creative energies lie in the self and not in the organizational strength of social forms.

❖❖

A Metaphysics of Individualism

CHARLES HARTSHORNE

"INDIVIDUALISM" has many meanings. By no means all of the attitudes or doctrines to which the term may refer are praiseworthy. Indeed some of them are great evils or blunders. "Each man for himself and the devil take the hindmost" is hardly a valid principle of action. But it could fairly be termed an individualistic maxim.

We are sometimes told that self-interest constitutes the final court of appeal provided the self is the true self, or the highest self. For in this true or highest self our nature as social beings will have its proper place. However, since death is the terminal state of every human self, and it is not apparent how anything is to my advantage when I am a corpse, self-regard can appear the final consideration only when we forget this universal law of our existence. If there is nothing beyond self-interest, then all sense of value is a head-in-the-sand affair, an illusion which should dissolve when we look around us in space-time. (The use of religious belief in a "hereafter" to circumvent this argument seems to me one of the most flagrant abuses to which religion has been put. To save egocentricity from its reasonable refutation through death is a sorry accomplishment to be credited to the love of God.) In addition, the doctrine is psychologically false. Love regarded as simply a means to the fulfillment of self-interest is pretended, not genuine, love. If to be happy we must much of the time forget ourselves, then we must really forget, and in doing so we cannot also be aiming at self-advantage. In addition, it is fantastic to try to prove that heroically giving up one's life for others is more advantageous to self in the long run than surviving for many years. Life on almost any terms is better than just nothing. Individualism as a theory of ultimate motivation is, I am convinced, a blunder, no matter how subtly the self be conceived.

A much better meaning of individualism is this: in each human person there is a certain degree of creative capacity. In every animal, indeed, there is, I hold, something of this capacity. To be an animal is to engage in decision making. To attribute behavior merely to instinct and stimuli is to trick oneself with words. Behavior does run in channels set by the past within and without the organism; but it does not follow that this dictates the details of behavior, any more than the banks of a river dictate the behavior of each molecule in the river. The banks set limits to anything like decision making by the molecules, but no physicist would undertake to prove that they remove the need for decision making on the molecular level. Physics has learned that nothing is gained by insisting upon classical causal determinism as an absolute. Psychologists should not make predictions of human behavior which surpass in confidence physicists' predictions for the behavior of molecules.

At this point I shall be reminded of the law of high numbers in probability theory, which, with the vast multitude of quantum phenomena in multicellular organisms, implies, it is argued, a virtually complete certainty for a given macroscopic outcome. But the assumption here is that quantum mechanics is strictly universal and subject to no qualifications when applied to living systems. Heisenberg has suggested that this assumption may well be unwarranted, and Wigner has also argued against it. On philosophical grounds I take the assumption to be false. It implies that the presence of experiences in a system makes no difference to its behavior (the laws of quantum mechanics have no variables corresponding to psychical conceptions), and I agree with Wigner that this assumption is quite unreasonable. As Whitehead says, there are no "idle wheels" in nature. Until *explicitly* psychophysical (psychophysiological) laws are added to physics, we are not entitled to consider our physical laws as universal in scope.

This does not mean that we must rest content with a dualism; on the contrary, it means, in my opinion, that all laws must finally be psychical laws. The ultimate science, if we are ever to have such a thing, must be a generalized comparative psychology, with physics the merely behavioristic aspect of such a psychology. In this generalized science of mind-behavior there would be many levels, and each level, e.g., the atomic, would be viewed behavioristically. Yet there would also be the imputation, in principle, of some form (however lowly or primitive in many cases) of awareness, feeling, memory, and the like. This, however, lies outside the present discussion.

The scientific defense of human creativity, genuine freedom, is not to be attained by making man a sheer exception, but by generalizing the principle at which physics has finally arrived, according to which strict regularities are in essence statistical and govern classes of occurrences, not occurrences taken one by one. This "Copenhagen view" has not been refuted. It holds that single microevents are not only unpredictable but objectively undetermined by their causal conditions. But if the microevents belong to a certain class (such as electrons in very low-grade or "inanimate" systems), then the law of high numbers applies, and we can get all the predictability we need. However, to identify a high-grade organism with a mere assemblage of microevents (each taken to be in itself exactly as it would be outside organic systems) is contrary to our direct awareness of the unity of each momentary experience. If we refuse to take this unity seriously, we shall no longer know what "unity" means, since unity in microevents is conceivable only by some sort of analogy with experienced unities.

In quantum mechanics, physics at long last appears to have got below assemblages to single events. The uncertainty "principle" is indeed a new principle (in physics). But like most discoveries it needs to be generalized. Instead, many of my colleagues in philosophy, and some scientists, have been energetically engaged either in trying to explain it away as a mere limitation to our knowledge, or in misusing the law of high numbers in order to restrict the application of the principle to microphysics alone. In short, they do not want it to be a principle, but merely another fact. Someone had to take that side, but is it hard to guess how such an argument will come out? Most theoretical physicists seem to expect the physics of the future to be even more rather than less different from the classical deterministic picture than quantum mechanics now is. Toward biologists or sociologists who bet the other way, my attitude is not exactly one of awe.

Incomparably more significant in man than in other animals—not to mention molecules—is the aspect of individual decision. For only to man do the alternatives for choice involve, in addition to trivial details of behavior, designs for living, ideals, religions, long-range objectives as well as short-range, and endless alternatives of symbolic, artistic, scientific, technological actions whose consequences can drastically affect all life on this planet. Since the essential dignity of man is in his symbolic power (speech, musical notation, graphs and diagrams, pictures, innumerable other forms of representation), every person who can effectively employ symbols of the human kind is to be recognized as qualified by this dignity. It follows that his right to a significant share in decision making must be acknowledged.

Here is the true meaning of "equality." Merely being in the shape of a human being is not the point: a simply idiotic person is only symbolically or ritualistically human in the value sense, not genuinely so, any more than a giraffe or a cow. But—you perhaps say—man and only he has an "immortal soul"? I wonder how you know that and know that while the congenital idiot has a soul, the kindly pet dog, equally intelligent, does not? I think we shall never agree upon a political equality which rests on no better foundation than the "immortal soul"—an idea which some distinguished theologians of our time view with misgivings as being more Greek or philosophical than Christian or religious.

The test of being human is ability to act humanly, and the critical factor is symbolic expression. This is why it has always been in principle mistaken to question the essential equality of the sexes and the races. No race or sex is known to be gravely handicapped from birth in ability to speak whatever language it is first exposed to, none is incapable of learning to interpret maps, musical scores, mathematical notations, pictures, pantomime—what you will. Hence all are well over the great divide between us and the subhuman creatures. Within each race or sex there are indeed persons who are not over the divide, and in these, as I have said, are only semblances of human worth, not the reality. There are also borderline cases whose classification is somewhat arbitrary.

Sometimes it is said that "one man is as good as another." "As good" in particular talents? This assertion would be hopelessly false, and it remains to a reasonable certainty quite false even if applied to the newborn infant and its potentialities. Genes are not fancies, and to deny that they must have important consequences for the development of skills seems egregious obtuseness—of which, I gather, a few sociologists, among others, have been guilty. "As good" in over-all, net human worth? And how is that to be measured or known? Does God perhaps think as highly of one human infant as of another? I have heard this said, but I fail to see any good reason why it should be said. Are we privy to the divine wisdom to that extent? My view is that it is no less presumptuous to pretend to establish the equal worth of all human individuals than to pretend to establish a definite hierarchy of worth among them. We should be more modest in both directions. There may well be great inequalities of over-all worth, but who among us is to judge of this? That there should be strict equality seems infinitely unlikely, and no one is the appointed judge of its obtaining in a particular case. Hence a man will do well not to claim to be "as good" as the other. The only valid claim is to be treated as human if one can act humanly, and to be accepted into the fellowship of essentially human animals with a reasonable share in the decisions by which our lives together are formed and transformed.

Decision making in important matters is not solely for official leaders. It is said (by one who may well know) that Mrs. Henry Ford at a certain juncture brought about a new policy toward labor in the Ford Company by informing Henry what she would do if he persisted in his previous policy. Again, any humble person might either cause or prevent a riot, under certain circumstances.

Concerning conformism and rebellion there seems little to add to the discussions in the other essays. No one rebels merely on his own, absolutely speaking. At least he is standing on the

shoulders of predecessors who did something more or less analogous; or he knows those who would be likely to do something
analogous; he has some feeling of tradition, or of support from
like-minded or partly like-minded associates; his language is almost completely given to him by others; perhaps his wife, or his
son or daughter, has trust in him, and so on. But it is important
nevertheless to keep in mind that human individuality is incomparably greater than that of any other terrestrial species. Granted
that the genes, taking them as the physically inherited individuality, cannot possibly of themselves determine adult behavior, they
also cannot possibly fail to influence it significantly somehow,
along with cultural factors. That the influence is important is beyond doubt, for the feeble-minded and moronic cases actually
render the cultural influence minimal. Moreover, there must, according to all analogy, be more subtle and less easily identifiable
but important effects. True, they are at present largely unknown.
We do, however, know that crime has genetic aspects. It is worth
realizing that crime is among the most compulsive, least creative,
modes of action.

To call a man a great man or a genius need not be taken to
imply that his genes were or are great or "genial." Genius or
greatness is not necessarily, or even probably, in any simple sense
inborn. Rather, a favorable, lucky constellation of original physical and early environmental factors makes possible or probable
the development of genius or greatness. This all seems truistic,
and I wonder that anyone disputes it. That actual greatness is not
simply inborn is an old doctrine, expressed by Gray in his lines:

> Some mute, inglorious Milton here may rest,
> Some Cromwell guiltless of his country's blood.

In other words, the genes were favorable to an important role,
but the cultural, including economic, factors were not. I can

imagine no plausible way in which this view, vague enough, to be sure, could be far wrong.

However, I flatly disagree with anyone who thinks that the genes plus all environing circumstances and past history simply determine behavior. This is taking a human organism to be less individual in its behavior than even a molecule or atom is known to be! By "individual in behavior" I mean precisely that any strict laws applicable to the behavior must be taken as statistical just so far as they are precise. For all we can ever know, at least, this principle is true even of the constituents of inorganic nature; much more of organisms. For they are more highly individuated, and this, according to the new principle, means that they depart more widely from the norm or law of their class. The departures being in all directions, uncoordinated, the law of high numbers applies, but the numbers are less high, and above all the human importance of the unique case is much greater.

Individuality means creativity, and "laws of creativity," other than statistical ones, are, I hold, a contradiction in terms. Why? Because to create, in the primary meaning of the term, is to add to the definiteness of reality, to close an antecedently open question, to add a new determination to the indeterminate but determinable antecedent universe. The doctrine of determinism, taken strictly, denies any such new determinateness. It views a happening as already completely predefined in its antecedent causes, each state of the world containing in effect an absolute map of all subsequent and all previous states, though man will perhaps never be able to read the maps except in radically incomplete and inaccurate ways.

I question if determinists can have much imagination, or having it, can really be using it when they theorize on this question. For if they did, they could hardly fail to see the fantastic nature of their doctrine much better than most of them seem to. So far from the view being eminently rational, because allegedly it makes all happenings completely explicable in principle, the view in truth makes all happenings in principle wholly inexplicable. Each phase of the "map" must have some sort of perfect isomorphism with every other, and this relation implies an ultimate yet quite definite or particular pattern of things which has always been just as it is now. And what is the explanation of the pattern —why the world has, or how it came to have, this pattern and no other? The determinist has rather few possibilities here, none of them in my opinion intellectually attractive. He may say there is no explanatory derivation of the ultimate pattern—period. He may say (with Spinoza) that it is the only possible pattern. He may say (with some theologians) that a supreme power eternally or originally chose the pattern once for all, either as the "best possible," or quite arbitrarily. I shall not take space to argue against these options; to me they are all rather silly. They are pseudo explanations. But determinism implicitly commits one to the disjunction among these views, all repellent when carefully examined.

Indeterminism can give a genuine, even though partial, explanation of the particularity of the world. Like all explanations of arbitrary facts, it is a genetic or historical one. The world is in the state it is because it gradually developed into that state: the immediately preceding situation made the present one causally *almost inevitable*, but not quite, leaving fine details to be settled in and by the events themselves as they happen. This self-determination in the present event by that event is freedom in the ultimate sense. Such self-determination does require causal conditions; the freedom in question is not in principle self-enclosed or absolute (this being a vacuous notion), but is in principle relative. It is freedom as to *how* to relate the present event or act to its immediate predecessors. This relatedness appears in our own experiences as memory and perception. The only freedom is as to *how* we shall remember, perceive, and evaluate the immediately preceding state of ourselves and our world. What is there to be remembered or perceived no one is free to decide; he is free only as to how, in remembering or perceiving, he responds to it. His sense organs largely dictate his perceptions of immediately preceding events outside his body. Precisely how his experience takes the final messages in the sense organs, puts them together with memory of what a fraction of a second before was his own experience, and, with the messages in all the other sense organs of his body and in the brain cells, out of this vast multiplicity of causes or stimuli makes a single complex experience—this is something which must, I hold, transcend the entire causal picture and add a new unit of determinateness to the world, a unit not quite distinctly represented in any previous causal map whatsoever, not even one which deity could decipher. In this I am agreeing with Bergson, Lequier, Peirce, James, Whitehead, and still other philosophers and scientists. The next moment this new unity is among the causal conditions for all future events. This view goes as far to explain particularity as any view whatever, and farther than any deterministic view. Particularity, definiteness, is *created* bit by bit, endlessly, and must not all be read back into the past as though it had always been there. Every strict, unqualified "preformationism" is false, no matter how crude or how subtle its formulation.

In the creation of reality, man has a larger role than other animals on this planet (not, I devoutly hope and believe, than all other animals). However, this does not in the least mean that one must accept a doctrine of soul-substance. James's analysis of the self into a process and a sequence rather than a strict identity is not only compatible with a lively belief in human creativity; it is the best way to express that belief. For the first result of creative freedom must be a new self for each moment. If my present act is to be really creative, my previous individuality must no more dictate the act than must anyone else's individuality. Self-determination must be *in* and *by* the present (though *for* the future and relative *to* the past, including the personal past). Thus, strictly speaking, there is a new "soul" each moment. This theory of a sequence of momentary selves was James's doctrine, and in this he knew what he was saying. After all, how could mere self-identity explain freedom? Identity implies continuing to be the same entity. If so, when I was born I was already what I am now, and it follows that I cannot have created anything in myself in the meantime. And if not in myself, then not in anyone else, for others, too, must be simply the very entities they were at birth.

It is, to be sure, common sense that events happen "to" things or persons. But Mahayana Buddhists long ago showed how this way of speaking can be translated into a language of events which dispenses with "things" or "persons" as primary concepts, though not as convenient shorthand devices. Here, too, physics seems to have come, in its own way, to this conclusion. An electron, we are told, is not a substance, whatever it may be. If, then, it is anything objective at all, it must be a kind of event. To say that events happen "to" something or someone means simply, in "event" language, that they fit into well-ordered, unbroken sequences of the sort we term "things" or "persons." However, the physicists now claim to have shown that in the microrealm we cannot dispense with the idea of events which do *not* fit neatly into any such sequences. In Whitehead's terms, these events have a low degree of "social" or "personal" order. But the existence of conscious minds consists in a high degree of such order, and no such minds could exist (the reasons are quite definite) save in organisms themselves highly ordered.

That the concept of substance, taken seriously and literally, is an intellectual prison can be illustrated in numberless ways. Consider, for instance, the contention that it is unscientific to talk about the individual "in last analysis" making culture, because it is culture that makes individuals. There are strong arguments for this contention. Yet what is culture if not certain things which individuals do to themselves and other individuals? All parties to such disputes assume too easily that "identity" through time is no problem. To add "culture," as identical through time, to individuals as persistent identities is not sufficient. What is really "in last analysis," or on the most concrete level, present in social reality is neither culture nor individual people but certain relatively ordered events characterized by a high level of symbolic functioning and creative freedom such as is found on this planet only in those event sequences which we call human beings. Each such event is intimately dependent upon and, except for a final and in many respects very minute aspect of self-determination, causally determined by events which have gone before. These include especially other events of a similar human kind, both within and without the individual sequence, exhibiting language habits and other customs, and embodied in such inanimate event sequences as buildings, tools, books, totems, flags, and so on and so on. The individual is indeed a product, something made, and the concrete making is not by the individual but by de facto members of individual sequences. Individuality is not the last, most concrete term of analysis. Neither is culture, though it may for some purposes be a more useful abstraction than "individual."

Our whole Western tradition is warped and confused by the concept of the individual taken as ultimate or concrete. The bad effects are ethical and not just theoretical. Nor, as I have argued elsewhere, is the issue irrelevant to the Cold War. The ignoble side of our "noble individualism" is very much with us, and is aided and abetted by metaphysical confusions about the relations of events to enduring things.

The individual who acts creatively now is not I, or you, as always the same entity, but I now, or you now. I yesterday, you yesterday—these did not perform or possess, and can never perform or possess, today's actions or experiences; only today's selves can do that. Yet, since there is a new agent each tenth of a second or so, the actual momentary freedom cannot be very large. At a given moment, we are almost entirely a product, not a producer. What productive power we have would be totally vacuous without inheritance from past actions—our own and those of countless others.

Similarly transcendent of individual identity is any rational motivation. Even to want to be appreciated and loved is in part to value others for their own sakes. Would one equally wish to be praised by a robot, even a practically very helpful one, as by a human being? Also, any future self, call it mine or not mine, which can benefit from my present act will be numerically a new and distinct unit of concrete reality. Hence mere self-interest, taken as absolute, has no realistic metaphysical basis. No wonder, perhaps, that the "event" philosophy is unpopular. Do we not prefer to cherish our ego illusion? Only Buddhism, by specializing in combating this illusion through a whole way of living, could popularize its overcoming, and even then hardly in a whole society.

Alas, the metaphysical baselessness of theoretical selfishness does not mean that metaphysical truth makes saints of those who discern it. Ethical issues are more concrete than the choice between accepting and rejecting pure selfishness. Absolute selfishness is nonsense, and it is worth realizing that this is so. But each person must still incline to take himself and his intimates more seriously than he takes human beings in general. Think of men who advertise cigarettes (and legislators who permit them to do this), because one can always demand even more conclusive proof than is yet available that cigarettes are killing multitudes of men and women. (Written before the report of the Surgeon General.) Are these manufacturers being merely selfish? Of course not. First of all, they are giving people what they apparently want, danger or no danger. No one is forced to buy. And the manufacturers and advertisers themselves smoke, thus sharing any risk. Also, they have families and employees whom they justifiably want to be able to provide for and investors to whom they want to yield a return; they have pride in their business, loyalty to their partners. One can scarcely live without some such concrete motivations as these. We could choose many other examples, and sooner or later the writer or the reader would be hard hit. Such is man, a monstrously confused mixture of motives. How much would it help if purely theoretical inquiries such as metaphysics would stop giving aid and comfort to the actual and harmful, but only relative, selfishness of people? Who knows? One would think it might help some.

Another example: think of millions of people who have put off getting automobile seat belts long, long after the evidence has become sufficient that to drive without them is to impose a substantial added risk upon passengers. No doubt this delay is partly just obtuseness, but how much must it not be shrinking from the trouble, or the cost, or the fear of being thought queer or morbid? Analyze it as you will, lack of concern for the welfare of others is surely an element, along, to be sure, with lack of concern, at a crucial point, even for one's own welfare. This last point illustrates the actual relativity, rather than metaphysical ultimacy, of individuality and individual self-interest.

This subject is in some aspects too sad and tragic for prolonged scrutiny, so far as I am concerned. If there is no original sin, there is something not obviously less awful, and it was never more apparent than now. But a metaphysical basis for self-interest in an idea of absolute self-identity as final term of analysis sheds no light on the terribly real *relative* validity, as secondary derivative concepts, of the notions of self and self-advantage. That the later members of a personal event sequence are normally of special concern to a given member is fully explained by the factors comprised by their membership in this sequence, and so is the special concern one feels for friends, family, close associates, explained by the very meanings of these terms.

On the other hand, larger groups, like nations, can survive only by inducing at least a minimal loyalty, which may clash with the more intimate relationships. And beyond all this, man is the metaphysical animal, who raises the absolute question: what is the standard beyond all other standards, the purpose beyond all others, the cosmic and everlasting measure of value? Whatever this standard may be, it is not the human individual, nor yet the human group either. These are values themselves requiring measurement. Neither self-interest nor even altruism in the ordinary sense can be final. The other selves, too, are secondary and ephemeral. Events are real, and enduring individuals are only events seen adequately in their interrelations; but if events of the ordinary kind are the last word, then futility is also the last word. For events are transient, apparently all heading toward nothingness.

I close on a frankly religious note. I believe that only a personal yet cosmic life can be the final recipient of our achievements, the ultimate beneficiary by which their value is measured. It can be this recipient because it is the one experiential personal sequence without termination in death (which does not mean that it is immutable, but only that it is "incorruptible," as our ancestors, in their wiser moments, used to say) and because its perceptions and memories are alone fully adequate to the happenings in the world, able fully to grasp and evaluate their qualities, their richness of detail and beauty.

The feeling and idea of such a transhuman reference of values can, it seems to me, help in giving sense to the notion of the individual's taking a stand against the judgment of the group. He cannot make any judgments without being largely determined by the influences of other human beings, and he cannot be simply indifferent to their approval and disapproval. Admitting all this, he can still remain vividly aware that the one he finally wishes to please is no human being, and that the resolution of the indeterminacies is in reality neither something effected once and for all by the past and the causal laws nor something to be left simply to others or to the one above even laws, but is a responsibility in which he has a genuine even though minute share—a responsibility not finally to other men but to the cosmic individual. This vertical and partly self-determined or free relation to the superhuman gives moral responsibility and the obligation to think for oneself their ultimate meaning, provided one avoids two sad blunders: the masochistic blunder of supposing that the supreme creativity makes all decisions for us, leaving nothing but mechanical "obedience" as our portion, in short supposing that the supreme creativity is the only creativity (a contradictory though popular notion) ; and the presumptuous blunder of confusing one's own decisions with those of deity. With acceptance of this moral responsibility, and with the observation of these precautions, courage and daring without fanaticism may perhaps be attained.

INDEX

Genet, Jean: 127

genius: as explanation of invention, 15–16, 17; as "magical" concept, 38–42; basis for measurement of, 40–42; as genetic and cultural, 137–138

George, Lloyd: 75

Golden, Harry: 59

Goldenweiser, Alexander: on individual as first cause, 15; on individual in cultural change, 18; as individualist, 25

Gray, Thomas: 137

Great Man: social influences on, 21; necessity of, in cultural change, 21–22; individuality of, 22–23; as genetic product, 137–138; as cultural product, 137–138

Gutenberg, Johann: 46

Hale, Edward Everett: 70

Hamilton, Alexander: Whiggery of, 76, 77, 79, 81

Harding, Warren (President): 74

Harrison, Benjamin (President): 79

Hassan, Ihab: "radical innocence" of, 122, 123

Heckscher, Eli: on laissez-faire doctrine, 48

Hediger, Heini P.: on chimpanzee sexual behavior, 5

Heisenberg, Werner: 42, 133

Hemingway, Ernest: isolation of heroes of, 119; mentioned, 127, 128

Hofstadter, Richard: 103

Hoover, Herbert (President): progress theory of, 82; on collectivism in New Deal, 84; as rugged individualist, 103; mentioned, 85

Hume, David: 54

individual: symboling ability of, 7–8, 134; in cultural developments, 9–10, 13–14, 13 n., 15–24, 39–42, 49–50, 142; as doer, 14–15; as inventor, 15–17; reality of, 13, 26–27, 28–29, 30; source of ideals of, 20 and n.; relation of race to, 24–25; emphasis on, in anthropology, 12–13, 24–26; as stop-thought word, 38; extreme, nature of, 52, 70–71; economic contacts of, 58–61; equality of, 95, 135–136; cosmic, as measure of value, 145–146. SEE ALSO individualism

—, behavior of: effect of experiences on, 10–11, 133; decision-making in, 132, 134, 135, 136; motivation of, 143–146. SEE ALSO creativity; individual, as determined

—, concepts of: culturological, 6–24 *passim*, 29–31; anthropocentric, 12–32 *passim*; genius, 15–16, 17, 38–42, 137–138; Great Man, 20–23, 137–138; meaninglessness of, 36–38; animism in, 42; as "process," 70, 114–115, 118–119, 140–141; as substantial self, 114–115, 140–143 *passim*, 145; as event sequences, 139–143, 145–146. SEE ALSO individual, as determined; self-assertion

—, cosmic: as measure of value, 145–146

— as determined: by cultural influences, 8–24 *passim*, 29–30, 44, 70, 137–138, 142; by biological influences, 8–9, 137–138; by self, 13, 139–140, 141; nature